WE'RE
BRITISH,
Innit

WE'RE BRITISH,
Innit

AN IRREVERENT A–Z OF
ALL THINGS BRITISH

IAIN AITCH

Collins

Collins
An imprint of HarperCollins Publishers
77-85 Fulham Palace Road
London W6 8JB

www.collins.co.uk

Published in 2008 by HarperCollins Publishers Ltd

Reprint 10 9 8 7 6 5 4 3 2 1

A catalogue record for this book is available from the British Library

ISBN-13 978-0-00-727132-0

Design and typeset by seagulls.net
Printed and bound in Great Britain by Clays Ltd, St Ives plc

Mixed Sources

Product group from well-managed
forests and other controlled sources
www.fsc.org Cert no. SW-COC-1806
© 1996 Forest Stewardship Council

FSC is a non-profit international organisation established to promote the
responsible management of the world's forests. Products carrying the FSC
label are independently certified to assure consumers that they come
from forests that are managed to meet the social, economic and
ecological needs of present and future generations.

Find out more about HarperCollins and the environment at
www.harpercollins.co.uk/green

Contents

Introduction 1

Introduction

Whether we see ourselves in the misty mornings of George Orwell's describing, Bill Bryson's fondly mocking words, the photographs of Martin Parr or the characters of *Little Britain*, we Brits are always looking to work out who we are and to maintain our idea of what it is to be British. As an island race, this identity is of paramount importance to us, and one that we have literally fought to maintain over the years. Yet, ask any group of Britons what the ideas, characteristics or items that define the nation are and you will get myriad different answers. It could be fish and chips, a sense of fair play or simply the ability to form an orderly queue at the drop of a hat. Though those questioned are just as likely to pick up on our love of tea, our complete disdain for the metric system or our ability to rattle on endlessly about the weather. Whatever Britain is, it does not stay the same for long. We know what we like and we love our traditions, but we are also endlessly adaptable and willing to give things a go. How else do you explain the success of the chicken tikka massala or dado rails?

This A-Z of Britishness is an attempt to finally pin down what it is that makes us British in the twenty-first century, as well as allowing you to measure your character, loves and dislikes against what I feel is the most definitive list yet created. Think of it as a kind of Citizenship Test for those

who already hold a passport or as an alternative learning guide for those who wish to get their hands on one. This is the real Britain, not one filtered through the eyes of civil servants and politicians. This is the dictionary of the Britain that you know and love, whether you ever whisper those three little words to it or not. This is not the sterile Britain shown in the photographs of a pamphlet issued by Her Majesty's Stationery Office, rather this is the Britain that finds Barbara Windsor as inspiring as Winston Churchill, the Britain that is still mildly suspicious of the 'continental' quilt. It is the Britain that wept for Princess Diana yet thinks her brother is a bit smug, the Britain that knows that pub that shows the football on a dodgy satellite hook-up from Turkey. It is the Britain that keeps our manicured lawn so tidy by throwing the slugs over the neighbour's fence and the Britain that pays the babysitter in alcopops.

This being a list of all things British, it will of course contain a good degree of the humour that we have become noted for. Endlessly self-deprecating, the British sense of humour is a huge part of our make-up. The ability to laugh at ourselves during times of turmoil, tragedy and the wrong kind of snow is what keeps us going when things are at their darkest, which is generally during an August Bank Holiday. Often painted as a pessimistic 'glass half-empty' nation, we merely have a point of view that the rest of Europe and the world do not understand. After all, a glass half-empty means that it is probably someone's round. Cheers! Mine's a pint of Spitfire. They don't like it up 'em the Germans.

Naturally, musing on nationhood and Britishness brings up questions of nationality, nationalism, devolution and where we stand as this uneasy alliance of England, Scotland, Wales and Northern Ireland. Is the West Lothian question getting easier every year? And will the broadsheets soon contain pictures of gorgeous blonde twins who have answered it correctly? When are we Great Britain, when are we the United Kingdom and when are we the United Kingdom of Great Britain and Northern Ireland? One thing is for sure, and that is that we are Royaume Uni during the Eurovision Song Contest. This is the only time, apart from during a particularly good Euromillions rollover, when we are ever allowed to think of ourselves as a part of Europe as a whole. Camp disco and camper heavy metal, yes. Single currency and kilometres, no. Such is the complicated nature of Britishness.

Within these pages you will find reference to everything from the rolling hills to the rolling cheeses that descend them on a summer's day. There are the people who have a special place in our history and those who have a special place in our hearts. Then there are the sights, sounds and even smells that make Britain what it is. Some of you are bound to disagree with the final selections, but let's not fight about it. Or if we do then at least let us take our jackets off before we begin; after all we are not French. There is an email address at the bottom of the page where you can send your suggestions, condemn me for treason or simply send pictures of things that you think scream Britishness.

Though try not to send those pictures you took to 'just try out' your new digital camera. *Readers' Wives* is indeed included in this book, but that doesn't mean I want to see your partner spread-eagled on your DFS corner suite.

For variety, I have variously referred to the subject of this book as the United Kingdom, Britain, Great Britain and various derivations thereof throughout the book. But whichever term I have used I mean the same place: This Sceptered Isle, Blighty, the Queen's gaff. Our home.

Please send your suggestions for what I have missed to youidiot@britishinnit.com. The five most glaring omissions will be written up by me and included in the paperback edition of the book (and you will, of course, get a copy).

ALCOPOPS

Although originally an Australian import, the alcopop became very much a part of the British way of life during the youth alcohol crisis of the 1990s. Teenagers were simply not consuming enough booze, which alcoboffins put down to them not wanting to acquire a taste through beer, cider or Buckfast as their parents had done. The instant gratification generation was in danger of being lost to sobriety, thoughtfulness and good deeds, so the booze manufacturers simply added a 5 per cent alcohol content to the teens' favourite soft drinks. This allowed them to get hammered on familiar flavours and had the added advantage of allowing them to get their friends unwittingly drunk as well. The side effect of this increase in teen drinking was a correlating rise in teen pregnancy, ensuring that the pensions crisis may yet be averted. Plans to reintroduce milk to primary schools as a 3 per cent alcohol 'alcomilk' are merely rumours at the time of going to press.

ALE

If someone comes into your local pub (see PUBS) asking the landlord if his beer is alive, they are probably not some kind of extreme animal-rights type who only eats wind-fallen apples and keeps yeast as a pet. They are most likely a real ale enthusiast. An unkempt beard and enormous gut may be other clues to look out for, but nowadays more presentable human beings are enjoying the taste of our country's ales. There have even been unconfirmed reports that a woman ordered some in the Midlands last year. It is very easy to laugh at hardcore real ale fans. So let's stop for a moment to do that. Okay, that's enough. Ale is one thing we do fantastically well in Britain, but it has been largely usurped by the search for the ever-colder pint of lager, with drinkers in the south preferring something approaching a lager Slush Puppy over a beer they can taste. Real ale brewers don't help themselves by calling their brews Old Dogge Bollocke or giving it some name and back story that you need to have a PhD in naval history to appreciate.

ALLOTMENTS

Like a kind of poor man's golf club, the allotment has traditionally been seen as a place for a man to be out in the open air, away from his wife and amongst specialist equipment. The knitwear tends to be more downbeat, but there is the added advantage of a shed in which to store pornographic magazines, pipe tobacco and a bottle of something warming. Of course, allotments are also places

that can be used to grow vegetables and they are becoming popular once again with city dwellers as the trend for organic and local food grows. Allotments have been around since the eighteenth century, but they really came into their own with the advent of World War II and the Dig For Victory campaign, which encouraged Britons to grow their own food. Allotments are generally owned by local councils or by allotment associations, with the annual rent being fairly cheap. In big cities there are waiting lists for allotments, which also enjoyed a 1970s boom in popularity when *The Good Life* showed us that self-sufficiency might lead to the ability to make our own cut-price wine or the possibility of sleeping with Felicity Kendall.

AMATEURISM

Sport in Britain was initially divided upon class lines, with superior sporting character bestowed upon those who could afford to compete for the love of the game and those who took a wage being seen as belonging to the lower orders. This distinction can be seen in the naming of the famous Gentlemen versus Players cricket matches of the nineteenth century (see CRICKET). The Gentlemen were the amateurs and the Players were the professionals, which cast those good enough to play for a living as less-than-noble money-grubbing savages. This belief in the idea of amateurism being a more tasteful and morally superior pursuit has pervaded British society ever since, resulting in our propensity to have a go at any number of things rather

than commit ourselves to becoming proficient enough to excel in one. This spirit can be seen in our bank holiday rush to the DIY superstores, our love of gardening and our desire to visit Ann Summers of a weekend. The utensils from all three pastimes may be interchangeable, but some of these things really are best left to a professional.

ANTS

These tiny insects are very much a part of any British summer, be they invading your picnic, running through your food cupboards or being victims of childhood experiments in the garden. Brits see the appearance of more than three ants in one place as some kind of declaration of war (as we know that ants are the only creatures other than humans that wage wars and this brings out the combatant in us). Chemical weapons are purchased from a hardware shop, with the lightly dusted doorstep being doused with boiling water should any enemy ants be subsequently spotted. Children become the SS concentration camp doctors of the summer-long campaign against ants, melting them with magnifying glasses, trying to teach them to swim and seeing what happens when you introduce red ants to a black ants' nest. The hottest day of the British summer is always that which is known as Flying Ant Day. This is the day (usually in mid-July) when all flying ants hatch and the skies become black with the confused creatures. Ice pops are always free on this day. Just ask at your local newsagent.

APOLOGISING

I am sorry to bring this up and I know it seems a little rude, but we Brits are apologetic to the point of irritation. We are the only nation that offers an apology when someone stands on our toes, barges in front of us in a queue or when we have to send back food in a restaurant (after we have had a five-minute argument with our dining partner about whether it would be too impolite to do so) (*see* POOR SERVICE). This character trait has lead to us slipping behind in the field of commerce and innovation in recent years, with inventors often not wanting to seem boastful by telling all and sundry about their cure for cancer or knowing how to start their pitch for investment in their product that will cure world hunger without saying, 'I'm really sorry, but ...'.

THE ARCHERS

Rumty-tumti-tumti-tum, rumty-tum-tralala. These are the opening sounds of the show that keeps Britain in touch with our rural communities and Radio 4 listeners convinced that they would be able to deliver a piglet if the need were to ever arise in some kind of unlikely porcine life-or-death emergency. It is really good fun to refer to it as Britain's oldest soap opera when you encounter an avid listener. Many Radio 4 listeners see themselves as above soaps, thinking of them (probably rightly) as full of planes crashing into bisexual threesomes at the top of an already flaming boozer run by small-time crooks with improper diction and a confusing family back story that involves siblings appearing and then

reappearing with someone else's face (*see* EASTENDERS). The best bit about *The Archers* is spotting when some snippet of farming news or politics is slipped in, sounding like the kind of clanging, clumsy insert you may expect on North Korean radio. All farmhands speak in a subhuman grunt language, which is both scary and sexually arousing for regular listeners.

ARCHITECTURE
Britain is littered with glorious examples of historical architecture, from the spectacular St Paul's dome by Christopher Wren to the innovation of Charles Rennie Mackintosh as well as a historical array that stretches from Tudor houses to spectacular statement buildings by Norman Foster or Richard Rogers. When it comes to our homes, things are a little less exciting. The fact that we call anything designed after 1900 'modern' could explain our attitude, as does the realisation that most new houses are some kind of Tudor-Georgian-Victorian cocktail, with windows about the size of the defensive arrow slits in old castles. Ask most Britons what they think 'contemporary home design' is and they will probably tell you it is a house that comes with the satellite dish already installed.

ARGOS
The rich have Harrods and Harvey Nichols, the middle class have Habitat and John Lewis and the poor have Argos, which combines low prices, high security and tacky jewellery under one enormous roof. You can buy your Reebok Classics, Nike

tracksuit, sovereign ring (*see* SOVEREIGN RINGS) and pay-as-you-go mobile at Argos, as well as picking up a plasma screen and a PlayStation 3. In fact, if the store were to branch out into booze, fags and a bit of weed then there really would be no need for Britain's underclass to shop anywhere else. In fact, if we just built an Argos into the middle of every new estate, put high fences around the perimeter...sorry, where was I? Oh yes, they have a strange system of shopping, whereby you have to select your item from an in-store catalogue, pay at a till and then collect your goods elsewhere in the store. A bit like internet shopping without the internet and with more people in Burberry baseball caps (*see* BURBERRY) smoking on your way in.

ARISTOCRACY

This thoroughbred strand of our society is born to lead, rule and have no chin. The chin was deliberately bred out of the class when it was found to inhibit correct soup eating, shouting 'yah' really loudly and certain secret aristocratic sex rituals, the likes of which we can only imagine. The chin also stops the nose being able to get quite so close to the cocaine, for a clean, mess-free snort. Previously entitled to rule via hereditary seats in the House of Lords, the old aristocracy is giving way to a new financial aristocracy who buy their seats in the new 'more democratic' upper house. This leaves the old aristocracy more time to murder nannies, shoot stuff and drive around their land wearing tweed (*see* HARRIS TWEED).

ASBOS

The Antisocial Behaviour Order is not, as some think, a court order that means you must behave in an antisocial manner, like some magistrate-lead game of Simon Says. Instead, it is an order of merit awarded to those who have proven great skill in the pursuit of being an absolute twat. As sought after as a place on the New Year's Honours list or a military decoration, the ASBO is a sign you have arrived and done great works among your community, whether it be playing the same Kylie record over and over at ear-splitting volume or punching out anyone who looks at you slightly askance. Winners of ASBOs are given special privileges, which means that they do not have to work ever again. Employers are instructed to not take them on, even if they beg, as their place in society is beyond mere employment.

AUTUMNWATCH/SPRINGWATCH

An orgy of frolicking, foraging and fornication, this hidden camera television show lets us see what our wonderful wildlife is getting up to when we are off at work or tucked up in bed. This is fairly passable if you catch it once while eating your dinner from a tray on your knees, but watch it more than once and you may find yourself caring more about a family of ducks than is actually healthy for a sane adult. The topic is interesting though, so what may liven things up is having former Goodie Bill Oddie trade jobs with investigative blowhard Donal McIntyre. That way McIntyre can report on the problems of violence among

gangs of blackbirds while Oddie can hole up in a caravan on a Leeds housing estate, commentating on feral youth and the disintegration of society. 'Aw, look. Here comes one of our crackheads, I think...yes, it's Dean and is that Tracy with him? Yes it is, and she is carrying their new crack baby. Now over to Kate, who has just caught a lovely happy slapping in Aberdeen.'

BADGERS

Depending upon your point of view, these are either evil tuberculosis-spreading vermin that would eat a baby given half a chance or they are just bizarrely prehistoric-looking creatures that snuffle around woodlands at night eating worms. Some say that they could be as intelligent as dolphins, but as scientists traditionally like to have an early night no one has yet been able to put these claims to the test. Badger-baiting is a popular pursuit among inbred rural folk, who gather around badger setts shouting insults like 'Come on then, stripey!' before fleeing into the night.

BAKED BEANS

An essential part of the fried breakfast (be it the English, Scots, Welsh or Northern Irish variation), baked beans are very much a national favourite, so much so that supermarkets are often willing to sell them at a loss just to get customers in to their stores. They know that we cannot resist a can of beans for 7p, even if we know they are the ones scraped from the remains of truckers' breakfasts at

transport cafés on the M6. Also eaten on toast, jacket potatoes or with chips, baked beans are worth £300 million in sales per year in the UK. The cost in environmental terms of our taste for the saucy haricot beans is still to be measured, with invisible methane clouds said to hang over many greasy spoon cafés (*see* GREASY SPOONS) and most building sites.

BANDSTANDS

The discarded condoms, the crushed cans of lager and the remains of a joint on the floor: nothing says relic of an age gone by like a bandstand. These ornate structures were built in our town parks and on cliff tops, mostly during the Edwardian and Victorian era, to provide a focal point for musical appreciation by the masses. Sadly, though, the masses discovered Radio 1, record players and, eventually, MP3 players, all of which left the bandstand to the winos, hoodies (*see* HOODIES) and skateboarders. Some bandstands have enjoyed a revival of late, thanks mostly to local historical organisations.

BANGERS AND MASH

Like it's cousin, pie and mash, this traditional dish of sausages and mashed potato ensures that every Briton gets the necessary combination of protein and carbohydrate without too much excess of chewing or worry about what kind of organs lie within the meaty part of the meal. Often

served with onion gravy and a side serving of English mustard, bangers and mash is a staple dish in many pubs. If the pub you are in is a gastropub then you will be told all about the provenance of the sausages as well as the name of the farmer who grew the spuds. You will then be charged £12.95. Bangers are so called because they are fat sausages that are likely to split open with a bang as they are cooked. You can always tell a good banger chef by his terrible complexion, which should be marked by hundreds of splashes of scalding hot fat emanating from exploding sausages.

BATHS

One thing that we took from the Roman invasion was the enjoyment of baths, so much so that a home is now considered incomplete without one. Showers are all very well to use on a holiday abroad, but our economy relies upon the vast range of products we use to spice up the time we spend wallowing in our own filth and dead skin, from bath salts and bubble bath to scented candles and portable radios. Many Brits feel so at home in the bath they choose to end their life in it, often committing suicide upon hearing their football team's result on the radio or after calculating how much in debt they are due to all the money they have spent on scented candles and bath oils.

BEACH HUTS

While our Mediterranean cousins simply take a G-string and some Factor 30 to the beach, we Brits have all manner

of stuff we need to carry with us, from lilos to gas stoves and kettles. To save carrying this on every trip, and to provide somewhere to shelter from the inevitable rain, we have the beach hut, which is nothing more than a simple promenade-based shed. But in recent years these have become prime slices of real estate, with a beach hut in Southwold, Suffolk costing about the same as a commuter-belt terrace. Artist Tracey Emin famously sold her Whitstable beach hut to art collector Charles Saatchi for £75,000, though he didn't even get a spot on the promenade or a two-man dinghy included in the price.

THE BEATLES

Possibly our finest export product of all time, John Lennon, Paul McCartney, George Harrison and Ringo Starr put British culture at the top of the tree when they took the world by storm in the 1960s with their Liverpudlian accents and mop-like hair. Lennon outraged Americans by proclaiming the band to be bigger than Jesus, a statement that, ironically, lead to huge record sales as everyone rushed out to buy Beatles albums to burn. God got his own back on the band, though, by having Lennon gunned down in New York, morphing Harrison into a hippie bore and making Starr best remembered as the voice of *Thomas the Tank Engine*. Saving most of his ire for McCartney, God created the Frog Chorus and Heather Mills, knowing that Paul could not weather the embarrassment of both.

BED AND BREAKFAST

Where you see these words outside a hotel you know that you are guaranteed two things. These things are a bed and a breakfast. What they will be like is anyone's guess, but by law you will be obliged to say 'Lovely, thanks' when asked by the proprietor how you found either. Many B&Bs have modernised in recent years, with most installing indoor toilet facilities and ceasing the morning ceremony of slopping out. Others are said to have done some light dusting. Breakfast food will have carefully been selected from a vast array of local suppliers, though this is mostly because the eggs are cheapest at Asda, the bacon at Lidl and the sausages at Iceland (*see* ICELAND). Tinned plum tomatoes are a compulsory part of the breakfast, even though no one has used them in this way at home since 1974.

BEEFEATERS

These distinctively attired guards at the Tower of London (*see* TOWER OF LONDON) have the official name of Yeomen Warders, but they are much better known as Beefeaters by the tourists who photograph them. The Yeomen live in the Tower grounds with their families and some are responsible for the welfare of the Tower's ravens which, legend tells us, protect the landmark. The name Beefeater is thought to have come from the fact that their duties afforded them a generous amount of meat from the king's table back in the fifteenth century, when they would have first been guarding the Tower. This link with meat lead to the name and

likeness of a Beefeater to be used by a chain of grill restaurants, which serve steaks and fried chicken but are forbidden from serving raven.

BINGE DRINKING

What government ministers call 'a binge-drinking crisis' many of us simply call 'Friday night'. For generations the British have lived with licensing laws that were designed to make sure World War I munitions workers didn't roll up drunk each morning, which meant that we all drank steadily until about 10.30 pm and then tried to cram in another three pints before closing time at 11 pm. This bred a nation of drinkers who saw drunkenness as a guilty pleasure and downing pint after pint as two fingers up to the ruling classes. With the introduction of longer licensing hours, stronger beer, alcopops (*see* ALCOPOPS) and the chance to be on TV shows like *Pissed People Throwing Up 2*, the problem of binge drinking has become more visible. Back in the day, six pints of mild would make you want a nice sit down and possibly a pickled egg. But modern industrial-strength chemical lagers and energy drinks mean that those coming out of the pubs are wide awake and have energy to burn, which leads to fights. The artificial colours used in curry house favourites and kebab shop chilli sauce just add to drunken hyperactivity. The patron saint of binge drinkers is Kerry Katona. Legend says that if you see her face in the bottom of your glass then you will make it safely home and not be sick on your shoes.

BISTO

There is no British food, from kippers to haggis (*see* HAGGIS), which cannot be improved immeasurably by the addition of gravy. The basis of good gravy is Bisto gravy browning, though some lazy types do prefer the instant gravy mixes offered by the same manufacturer. Bisto did swear by its slogan 'Aah, Bisto' for some years, which was supposed to signify the olfactory joy of catching the scent of its gravy. This was later abandoned, however, when it became clear that the slogan was what school children were saying to one another when they had produced a particularly pleasing and pungent fart.

BLANKET

No picnic, car journey or bed and breakfast stay is truly complete without the blanket. This sometimes itchy sign of our defiance of all things European is our woollen riposte to that foreign invader the continental quilt, the very name of which implies a deep distrust. What other piece of knitwear could serve as lunch table, be used to warm a grandmother's knees and provide your bedding? We certainly didn't build an empire toting around something stuffed with goose feathers, and which required a 'tog rating', whatever that is.

BLITZ SPIRIT

Signifying our ability to simply get on with things under the most trying of circumstances, this term comes from our stoicism during the bombing raids of World War II,

especially those in 1940/41. As a nation on and under fire we pulled together, watched each other's back and, most importantly, made sure that everyone had a cup of tea on the go at all times. Filmmaker Humphrey Jennings directed a short film at the time called *London Can Take It*, encouraging unity and a general 'Is that the best you've got/you call those bombs?' attitude from the populace (*see* STIFF UPPER LIP). The call for the Blitz Spirit is often made in times of crisis, such as the July 2005 London bombing campaign, though some believe that this community ideal cannot be properly attained without the mass ingestion of powdered egg.

BLUE PETER

Very much the official BBC view of how children should be seen, *Blue Peter* has been an institution of British broadcasting since 1958. The show has always represented an idealised middle-class view of childhood, with its repertoire of craft activities, good works, animal husbandry and nature study. This all went along jolly nicely until the ITV network started to show *Magpie* in 1968, a programme that, if some middle-class parents were to be believed (*see* CLASS), was tantamount to Satanism. *Magpie* presenters just lolled around in a stupor, urging viewers to attack the Blue Peter garden, plant Sherbet Dib-Dabs on the BBC show's presenters and make them senselessly rig competitions to decide the names of pets. But it was *Blue Peter*'s optimistic altruism that dealt the show's ethics one of its greatest blows

when in 1981 it broadcast a short film about cerebral-palsy sufferer Joey Deacon. Within days, Joey mania had spread across the country, with children imitating Deacon's guttural attempts at speech and labelling anyone weak or different as a 'Joey'. The slang term persists to this day.

BLYTON, ENID

With hundreds of books written and hundreds of millions sold, Enid Blyton is probably Britain's best loved and most read author. Her writing may be considered dated and restricted, as well as occasionally racist and sexist, but you can be sure that more Britons have read her work for pleasure than have ever opened up those leather-bound *Complete Works of Shakespeare (see* SHAKESPEARE, WILLIAM*)* that languish on so many shelves. The *Noddy* stories are still extremely popular in book form and on television (though now stripped of the golliwogs), but it is the *Famous Five* and *Secret Seven* series that are the archetypal Blyton books that we Brits have a fondness for. These promise adventure, secret hideaways, idyllic child-hoods, swarthy strangers and lashings of ginger beer once the mystery is solved. Blyton claimed to have written entirely from her imagination, though if you consider the bizarrely fantastical content of some of her fantasy stories like *Folk of the Faraway Tree* alongside the fact that she wrote as many as 10,000 words per day then you could be forgiven for wondering what the hell she was putting in her tea.

BOAT RACE

Ostensibly a simple rowing race between two universities (*see* OXBRIDGE), this contest somehow clambered its way up the roster of sporting events of national importance to sit alongside the Grand National and the FA Cup Finals and became a regularly televised spectacle. The first race between Cambridge and Oxford universities' boat clubs was in 1829, with both teams being named 'blues' after the colour of their blood. The race is from Putney to Mortlake, which is 4 miles and 347 yards. The point of the race, for the general public at least, is that at least one of the boats should sink, though this has not happened in the actual race since 1978, when the light blues of Cambridge went under.

BOND, JAMES

The dashing MI6/Secret Intelligence Service agent, created by writer Ian Fleming in 1952, was named after the author of a book about birds he happened to have at his Caribbean home. The first Bond novel was 1953's *Casino Royale*, with the huge success of the series dictating that they be turned into films. The Bond film has been a hugely successful franchise since Sean Connery first starred in *Dr. No* in 1962, though Fleming himself saw actor David Niven as more the archetype of 007. Speculation over who the next actor to play Bond will be always makes for a large number of column inches in the press, with Daniel Craig being the current incumbent. Bond is known for his love of fast cars,

fast women and nifty gadgets. The Aston Martin DB5 is the classic Bond car, though the luxury motor manufacturers have never thought to market a model with a working ejector seat. The Bond film is always a favourite on television at Christmas: their simple plots and the likelihood that they will be repeated mean that even the most inebriated, unconscious member of the family can follow the story-line.

BOUDICA

Queen of the Iceni people in the east of England at the time of the Roman invasion, Boudica (or Boudicca or Boadicea) was one of the most fierce and fearless British women of all time: she was even scarier than a night out with Scary Spice, Pat Butcher and Anne Robinson. Boudica is famed for taking on the Roman forces and destroying Colchester, St Albans and the fledgling city of London, leading a rebel army in a fit of ransacking and destruction not seen on a similar scale until closing time on Oliver Reed's stag night (*see* STAG NIGHTS). Boudica was eventually defeated somewhere in the Midlands around 61 AD, though not before thousands on both sides had died. Fatalities are thought to have been fewer on Reed's stag night, though no accurate records for casualties on either historic occasion are available.

BOWLER HATS

For around 100 years from its invention in 1850, the bowler was the dominant British hat, transcending class headwear

rules and leaving an enduring image of the Brit as bowler-hatted. The hard felt hat was designed by James and George Lock and manufactured by the Bowler family milliners for the Earl of Leicester. The Bowler was initially used as a riding hat, though it soon became popular with bankers and civil servants, offering a halfway house between the top hat and the flat cap. The Bowler was later adopted by some manual workers, who prized its protective raised dome. It has largely fallen out of fashion now, though it did enjoy a resurgence in the late 1960s, thanks to the film *A Clockwork Orange*. This brief revival was most confusing, as you couldn't tell who was a slightly eccentric outmoded banker and who was a psychotic film fanatic bent on a bit of the old ultraviolence.

BOXING DAY

While the rest of the (Christian) world gets on with life as normal from about 5 pm on Christmas Day, we draw the whole thing out by adding Boxing Day on 26 December. The day is said to be when servants were given their 'Christmas box', usually some kind of bonus, by their employer, though its name may also be derived from this being the day when drunk or hungover members of the aristocracy were most likely to beat (or 'box') their charges. This tradition of fisticuffs on Boxing Day was continued by football fans, as the day saw local derby matches played between teams such as Liverpool and Everton as well as between Arsenal and Tottenham Hotspur. Fans of these teams still have songs in their repertoire that boast 'We

shall fight for ever more, because of Boxing Day'. I am sure that some families would be only too willing to echo those sentiments.

THE BBC
(BRITISH BROADCASTING CORPORATION)

Depending on your opinion (and mine depends very much upon whether they want to option this book as the basis for some kind of 'Best of British' style show where C-list celebrities pretend to remember clips they have just been shown), the British Broadcasting Corporation is either a wonderful British institution, the pinnacle of broadcasting and worth every penny of the licence fee or an overblown money pit that taxes viewing, wastes budget on endless clip shows and is a propaganda machine for Britain's politically correct liberal-left. The corporation was founded in 1922 by Lord John Reith and came into state ownership in 1927. Its mission statement slogan is 'Nation shall speak unto nation in quite a posh accent' (*see* QUEEN'S ENGLISH) and it is now responsible for a huge array of television channels, radio stations and internet sites across the globe. The BBC has been responsible for nearly all of Britain's best-loved radio (*see* RADIO 4) and television programmes, as well as *Noel's House Party*.

BRITPOP

Re-enactment societies have long been popular in Britain, often re-staging battles between the Roundheads and

Cavaliers or even the rival armies of World War II, though in 1997 it was a musical conflict that was re-enacted, with Britpop reliving the days when you had to choose between The Rolling Stones or The Beatles. Unfortunately, it all went a bit wrong when the media re-created the nonexistent battle of The Kinks against The Beatles between middle-class mockney band Blur and the faux Fab Four, portrayed by working class Mancunian monobrow merchants Oasis. Lots of Union Flags (*see* UNION FLAG) were waved, some other similar bands formed and took a large amount of cocaine, some stole bass lines from old punk bands, Tony Blair was elected and everyone got home in time for tea (*see* TEA AS A MEAL).

BRUSSELS SPROUTS

According to just about every poll ever taken, the Brussels sprout is Britain's most hated vegetable, which is going some as we really don't like vegetables all that much at all. Even the country's vegetarians are pretty ambivalent about veg. The correct way to cook brussels sprouts, or any other vegetable, is to score, soak for a week and then cook at a rolling boil for one hour. Don't pay any attention to what Nigella says, just because her dad used to be a really corpulent Chancellor of the Exchequer and is now really quite skinny; you don't want to risk your vegetables being *al dente* (which is Italian for recognisable). When Brussels sprouts are grey they are ready to serve. It is mostly the taste and gas-giving after-effects of these vegetables that we dislike,

but the fact that they bear the name of the Belgian home of the EU adds to our hatred, as this is the place that sneers at our apple varieties and wants to impose straight fruit standards upon our native banana growers.

BULLDOG

The British Bulldog is the animal that we see as most summing up the British spirit, reflecting our never-say-die attitude (*see* BLITZ SPIRIT), combative loyalty, tendency towards inbreeding and propensity to snore heavily. The slack-jowled canines are less aggressive than modern 'devil dogs' such as variations on the American pit bull, but they will stand their ground and match any breed when riled. The dogs also lend their name to the classic playground game British Bulldog, which is a kind of disorganised free-for-all licence to assault fellow pupils.

BUNTING

These distinctive decorative hangings are a sign of celebration and good times: the lengths of string and pieces of triangular cloth are hung across village streets, school fields or outside council offices. Most often used to mark a summer fête or a street party, bunting is usually red, white and blue, displaying a touch of patriotism. Bunting is also used to decorate used-car sales outlets, signifying that the secondhand car business is a non-stop party. Traders displaying bunting are obliged by law to blow one of those party streamers should you make a purchase.

BURBERRY

Founded in Basingstoke in 1856, Burberry grew to be one of Britain's best-known premium clothing brands, with its raincoats being seen by those at the top of society as the *de rigueur* thing to wear during a downpour, be it in Berkeley Square or in rural Buckinghamshire. Burberry invented the trench coat for the War Office at the start of World War I, as well as kitting out Armundsen for his South Pole mission. Its reputation as a fashion brand has lead to Burberry being one of the most bootlegged ranges in the world, with fakes featuring its distinctive brown and beige tartan fabric popping up on market stalls everywhere from Romford to Riyadh. The Burberry baseball cap has become the signifier of football hooligans and chavs (*see* CHAV), leading many bars to ban them and the brand to cease their manufacture. In 2006 Burberry closed its manufacturing base in Treorchy, South Wales, moved its operations to China and thus ceased to be a truly British brand. Ironically, counterfeit Burberry is often more British than the real thing now, with much of the fake designer wear being made on industrial estates in the Thames estuary area.

BURNS, ROBERT

To the Scots, Robert Burns is every bit as important as William Shakespeare as a literary figure. The poet wrote in English and in Scots dialect and is probably best known for writing the lyrics to *Auld Lang Syne*, which most of us can

just about half remember by the time we come to sing it each New Year's Eve. Burns died at the age of just 37 (from a rheumatic condition thought to have been worsened by prodigious drinking), though he left enough of a legacy to be celebrated each year on 25 January, when Scots and their descendants mark Burns' Night. This occasion sees Burns' *Address to a Haggis* (*see* HAGGIS) being read, which is followed by a large amount of haggis eating and whisky drinking. Robert Burns is in no way related to Montgomery Burns from *The Simpsons*, though he is celebrated in the United States by having two towns named after him.

CARAVANNING

Hated by pube-haired television petrolhead Jeremy Clarkson and loved by former foreign secretary Margaret Becket, caravanning brings the British characteristic of amateurism to holidaying. After all, why stay at a hotel when you can tow around a small tin can that contains a chemical toilet and a foldout bed? Most true caravan enthusiasts carry a small tartan flask with them at all times, so that the police can be sure they are not new age travellers or gipsies.

CARRY ON

This series of 30 comedic films ran from 1958 to 1978 (let's ignore 1992's mirthless disaster *Carry On Columbus*), creating a uniquely coherent documentation of British tastes, attitudes and humour throughout the period. The films were at their best from the mid-1960s to mid-1970s, containing a wonderful blend of self-deprecation, self-aggrandisement, saucy seaside humour, prudery, sex-starved wives, hen-pecked husbands, camp and red-blooded male

fantasy. Not every film hit the spot, but any that contained the mix of Sid James, Kenneth Williams, Charles Hawtrey, Joan Sims and Bernard Bresslaw was usually a winner. The series' finest moment came with *Carry On Cleo* in 1964, which was filmed on the set of *Cleopatra* and is memorable for the Kenneth Williams' line (as Julius Caesar): 'Infamy, infamy – they've all got it in for me.' Though Sid James (as Mark Antony) also manages to sum up the series' attitude to foreign languages with the simple expression 'Blimus!'. Another seminal (quite literally for boys who were reaching puberty at the time) *Carry On* moment was when Barbara Windsor's bra flew off during a workout in 1969's *Carry on Camping*, which is one of the best-known scenes in British cinema history.

CHANGING THE GUARD

The Queen (*see* QUEEN ELIZABETH II) is notorious for being easily bored, so most mornings she gets up, puts on her ermine dressing gown and screams, 'Won't someone change this bloody guard, I am bored of looking at them now'. This distractedness is fortunate for tourists, who love to see the pomp and ceremony as different regiments and companies hand over the keys for Buckingham Palace amid a display that reflects the very best of British tradition. It is colourful, dramatic and rather baffling for all but those taking part. More baffling still is the retention of the mounted Queen's Life Guard on Horse Guards. These mounted troops sit in place for most of the day,

ready to save the Queen should she be involved in a swimming accident, despite there having been no swimming facilities in the immediate vicinity since the time of the reign of Queen Victoria (*see* QUEEN VICTORIA). On hot days the Queen has been known to feign distress in a small inflatable paddling pool, just to make sure that the Life Guard are paying attention.

CHAV

Origins of this shorthand term for white working-class youth are much disputed, with everything from Romany, Geordie and Kentish slang offered up as the true source of the name given to this group that mostly shops at JD Sports and considers a trip to Matalan as 'a bit posh'. Male chavs mostly don tracksuits, trainers and Nike or (fake) Burberry baseball caps, while the female of the species often scrapes her hair back in the tight 'Croydon face lift' style, usually teaming WAG fashion items with something in white polyester to show off her fake tan. Confusion has reigned in town and country since male chavs started to adopt expensive outdoor wear brands such as North Face and Berghaus, especially as the latter was previously worn mostly by over-60s on rambling outings (*see* HOODIES; RAMBLING). This strange brand appropriation can cause great consternation when seeing an anorak-clad group approaching, not knowing whether they are going to drunkenly harass you or offer you some Kendal Mint Cake.

CHEESE ROLLING

The summer months do odd things to us Britons, bringing out our pagan past and our desire to mark the season with odd festivals, strange sporting events and suicidal chases after things we could quite easily buy at Tesco (or Waitrose at the very least). The end of spring and approach of summer sees grown adults, some with no known history of mental impairment, taking part in shin-kicking contests, toe-wrestling bouts and the annual cheese rolling at Cooper's Hill in the Cotswolds. In this contest a whole Double Gloucester cheese is released to bounce its way down the hill, with actual human bipeds following it after a one-second gap. As the cheese reaches terminal velocity those following smash into each other, into the hillside and into the fence at the bottom of the hill. Broken limbs are usual. Catching the cheese is not. All of this adds to the world's view of us as lovable eccentrics (*see* ECCENTRICITY), though few are willing to acknowledge our prowess in this kind of sporting pursuit, which is why they are objecting to shin-kicking and racing with a burning barrel of tar on your back being included in the 2012 London Olympics.

CHIPS WITH

Yes, we do eat chips with almost everything in the UK, but there is a special place in our heart for the takeaway tradition of smothering the delicious golden fingers of potato in a variety of toppings. The law of the chip shop says that only four are acceptable: these are gravy, curry, peas, or

beans. Of course, the peas must be mushy and the beans must be of the baked variety, though curry and gravy allow for more vagaries. Should it be thick? Should it be runny? Should the curry be a strange green colour and have raisins in it? Probably not. Some modernists seem to believe that cheese is also an acceptable topping, but these people are just wrong, sick even. If you are one of them please seek help. These wonderful meals should always be eaten from a polystyrene tray while walking, using a wooden fork that is far too small to be of any practical use and offering the very real risk of planting a two-inch splinter in your tongue.

CHURCH BELLS

The quintessential sound of morning in a British village is the peal of the church bells, calling worshippers to prayer, annoying shift workers and those with a hangover equally. The patterns of ringing do not vary much, becoming such a part of our national soundtrack that we will notice any irregularity. The language of the bells was utilised in civil defence plans during World War II, with different tolls meaning that the Germans had landed. This can be seen in effect in the 1942 film classic *Went the Day Well*, where rural villagers are inspired to a spiffingly jolly killing spree when Nazi infiltrators choose to invade their village and their village alone. The extended ringing of bells is mostly associated with the end of a wedding, which really is the last thing you need if you are still suffering the effects of your stag night.

CHURCHILL, WINSTON

Widely regarded as one of Britain's greatest leaders and often pictured on a Union Flag background giving his distinctive two-fingered salute, Winston Churchill has become the standard by which other Prime Ministers are measured. Churchill is famed for his leading of the UK through most of World War II, serving as Prime Minister of an all-party group from 1940-1945, with a second term as Conservative Prime Minister from 1951-1955. Often seen with cigar in hand, it was Churchill's skills in speechmaking and in soundbites that kept British spirits high during the war years (*see* BLITZ SPIRIT). Turning adversity to strength, his speeches such as his pre-Battle of Britain one which included the line 'We shall fight them on the beaches' are still remembered to this day by many. Chamberlain saying 'Oops, this has all gone a bit tits up' may not have had the same rallying effect. Sadly, most school children now think Churchill is 'that dog in the insurance adverts, innit'. There is some irony in this, as Churchill suffered from depression, a condition he referred to as his 'black dog'. If he had known his memory was to be overshadowed by an animated nodding bulldog then his black dog may have come visiting more often.

CHURCH OF ENGLAND

For many years this was the default setting with which all Britons were born; the Church of England is the religion for people who don't really do religion. Often shortened to C of

E to do away with the overly religious overtones of the word 'church', it is the religion you can enjoy between worships without ruining your agnosticism. Mostly there for christenings, weddings and funerals, your C of E vicar is always up for attendance at village fêtes, tea dances or jumble sales (*see* JUMBLE SALES). A surprising 37.3 million of us identified ourselves as Christian in the 2001 census of England and Wales, vastly outnumbering the 3.7 million who claim to have no religion and the 390,000 who adhere to the Jedi faith. Hopefully, state-funded Jedi faith schools should be introduced within the next decade.

CIDER

With Britain's wealth of orchards it is no surprise that we soon worked out how to turn apples into a passable alcoholic drink, which has kept tramps, teenagers and farmers topped up since time immemorial. Premium ciders enjoy massive sales, but the real stuff comes from the West Country, where everyone talks, drinks and sings like The Wurzels. Popular brands have fantastic names like Cripple Cock, with a slippery slope of rough cider and scrumpy available to explore in rural boozers. One of the best things about cider is that many Americans use the same name for what is simply apple juice. So when a coach party stumble across a cider outlet in Bristol they are always tempted to try the local beverage, not realising that they are imbibing an 8 per cent brew that will have them under the table. This is the best time to tell them about the 'tradition' of visitors buying a round for the whole pub.

CIVIL SERVICE

With its name deriving from the Latin for 'to lose documents and mislay CDs full of data', the Civil Service is the backbone of British bureaucracy. Its stated purpose is to retain as much of your money as possible while also making it nigh on impossible for you to claim any of it back in times of need. The Civil Service includes the Government departments that deal with taxation, social security and prisons, though its name is most often linked with the administration and running of the Government itself, with Whitehall's civil servants being some of the most powerful employees in the country. Despite having the word 'civil' in its title, the Civil Service does not insist on civility being a requirement of its staff when recruiting. In a 2002 survey only 14 per cent of civil servants surveyed identified as mildly to reasonably civil, whereas 45 per cent responded by simply hanging up the phone after leaving those asking the question on hold for 20 minutes.

CLASS

Foreign visitors are amazed by it, politicians claim it no longer exists and the rest of us struggle to work out where we belong within it. The class system in Britain is second only to the Indian caste system in terms of rigidity and complexity. Our place of birth, parent's jobs, income, accent and even what we call our evening meal (*see* TEA AS A MEAL) can dictate our place on the class scale, which can then affect education, career and even marriage. Within the

confines of working, middle and upper class there are any number of micro-classes, such as lower-middle or Duke of Cornwall, though it is hard to be mobile even between these. Jumping class boundaries is notoriously difficult: moving from working to middle requires acquiring a taste for olives and houmous, while middle to upper means knowing which fork goes where and which servant should polish them. Class envy is one thing that is upwardly as well as downwardly mobile, with the middle classes often affecting working-class accents to fit in. This is most in evidence when they have to call out a plumber and constantly refer to him as 'mate', even though he actually earns twice their salary.

COMMONWEALTH

Formed from the ashes of the British Empire (*see* EMPIRE), the Commonwealth is a grouping of 53 nations that come together to discuss and promote common aims around matters such as law, trade and peacekeeping. Additionally, this gives us in Britain something to feel in charge of, as well as bringing together a set of nations that we have some hope of beating in sporting pursuits. Our Queen is the current head of the Commonwealth, as well as head of state of some of the Commonwealth nations, such as Canada, Australia and New Zealand. These countries have been retained in this way as they are some of the tougher Commonwealth nations to beat at the Commonwealth Games and the Queen can simply order them to throw races or matches as she sees fit.

CONSTITUTION

In Britain, we have an unwritten constitution. This works in much the same way that unwritten homework or an unwritten note from your mum to get you out of PE does, in that it does not exist and is therefore pretty much worthless. For example, this means that any old dictator can come along and say 'Don't you remember? Killing of the firstborn is part of the unwritten constitution. I am reading it now, in my head.' There have been many calls for a written constitution or Bill of Rights, but these things are always best agreed upon when a society is in its infancy. Once a country has evolved towards having reality TV shows and worshipping Graham Norton then you just know that the whole thing would be decided in a lengthy vote at primetime on BBC1. Sensible clauses would be voted out in week three, only for ones like 'the right to visit the corner shop shirtless' (*see* CORNER SHOP) and 'the right to urinate in public swimming pools' ending up as irrevocable law.

COO-EE

This homely greeting is mostly used by ladies of a certain age, usually to call across to a friend who is toting a wheelie bag or zipping by on a mobility scooter. Often called at frequencies that are inaudible to male ears, a call of 'coo-ee' can simply mean hello, though it will often be a prelude to an invitation for cake. As everyone knows, British old ladies spend a good amount of time refining and re-refining their fruitcake recipes and this word can act as a code or boast

about a particularly fine cake. If you are lucky enough to hear this call then be ready to follow, as it could lead to a secret cake sale, which is kind of like the old lady equivalent of the underground rave scene.

COOKING LAGER

With the spread of pub chains, the growth of vertical drinking establishments and the pressure for breweries to maximise profits, what was once considered an exotic, premium drink has fallen to the very bottom of the heap. This means that standard strength lagers with identikit flavours are now referred to as 'cooking lager' rather than by the overseas brand names they bear. Cooking lager is usually brewed in the UK under licence and is the drink for those who have abandoned all hope that their drink will taste of anything at all. They don't need to ask for it by name, all they want is the worst lager the house has available. Still, at least it is preferable to the 'wife-beater' sobriquet that one premium brand has acquired among drinkers.

COOL BRITANNIA

Inspired by the resurgence of British music and fashion, as well as the changing mood of the country in the run-up to the 1997 Labour Party General election win, Cool Britannia was a handy media tag that encompassed anything that was on the up in the UK at that time. US magazine *Vanity Fair* summed up the time with the Carnaby Street-inspired headline 'London Swings Again!', naming designers such as

Alexander McQueen and artist Damien Hirst as prime examples of what was cool about Britain. The cover of the magazine featured celebrity incubator Patsy Kensit sprawled on a Union Flag bedspread with Liam Gallagher. Cool Britannia even made Geri Halliwell look good, with a million middle-aged men committing to memory the image of her in *that* Union Jack dress. Sadly, the sham fad lasted for less time than the average Kensit marriage and was over by the time Tony Blair was breaking manifesto promises.

CORNER SHOP

No British community is complete without its corner shop. The shop need not actually be situated on the corner of a street to be considered a corner shop, but it should provide the focus for a community by providing overpriced items that you may have forgotten to pick up from the out-of-town superstore. Principal among these items are Pringles, bourbon biscuits, cigarettes, pornographic magazines and bizarre cakes you never see anywhere but in corner shops. Often run by Asian immigrants and their families, some corner shops are still known as 'Paki shops' by those locals whose knuckles drag along the pavement as they walk. This tendency towards casual racism and the linking of Asian families to these stores was acknowledged by British-Asian band Cornershop in their choice of name. The band's tour rider consisted mostly of firelighters, out-of-date boxes of Milk Tray chocolates and Lemsip.

CORONATION STREET

This reality television series about life in northwest England has been running since 1960, giving the rest of Britain a fly-on-the-wall look at the small suburb of Weatherfield, where simple pleasures such as adultery, murder, abduction and having a pint in the Rovers keep the mostly working-class populace happy. Teacher Ken Barlow has been featured in the show since it began, but residents have come and gone over the years, with most getting to sample Betty's hotpot in the pub and sex with Ken's wife, Deirdre, though never at the same time (at least not yet). Most fans will have their own view of what constitutes classic 'Corrie', though many name motormouthed harridan Hilda Ogden as their favourite character.

CRICKET

The sound of leather on willow and the long shadows on county grounds are often cited as being two of the things that most evoke an image of Britishness, though cricket is really most popular in England, where the sport was invented. It is thought to have been around in the southeast since the fourteenth century in some form, though the development of the cricket tea and the five-day test came somewhat later on. The modern game was given nobility and popularity in the nineteenth century by cricketing legend W G Grace, who is as famous for his lustrous beard as for his skills as a batsman. In recent years the cricketing authorities have tried to sex the game up by introducing ever-shorter matches, but

true fans enjoy the endurance and possible letdown of the five-day game, where hours of nothingness are interrupted by the most fleeting moments of action. Watching such a game is as close as the average British male ever comes to a state of Zen, though this is often aided by several pints of lager. Those unable to attend big games should listen in to Radio 4, where commentary on the game is squeezed in between audio clips of elderly men eating cakes.

CRICKET TEST

The cricket test, as opposed to test cricket, is derived from a question posed by former MP Norman Tebbit in a 1990 interview with the *LA Times* newspaper. He asked who second-generation immigrants would support in sporting competitions, stating his belief that many would 'fail the cricket test' by rooting for Pakistan, India or the West Indies over England. Tebbit saw this test as an indicator of how British immigrants and their descendants felt, despite the fact that most of Scotland would also root for any of those nations over the English team. Then there is the fact that those of Indian heritage will cheer for England when they play Pakistan, with those of Pakistani origin doing the same when England are up against India. Tebbit claimed vindication of his views when homegrown suicide bombers attacked the London transport system in July 2005, though it seems unlikely that a lengthy interrogation about their views on Freddie Flintoff would have stopped the terrorists from carrying out their mission.

CRUMPETS

As with most baked goods in the UK, there is an almighty bloody row just bubbling beneath the surface over the naming, appearance and origins of crumpets. Some say they are those things with holes in that look like a circular bath sponge, which you cover in butter, jam or something savoury, but others say that they are thin and floppy – more kitchen scourer than sponge. Those in the Midlands confuse matters further by calling anything vaguely crumpet-like, a pikelet. I mean, can't we all just get along? Crumpet is also slang for an attractive woman, though the word is now more associated with the attractive older woman. The phrase 'thinking-man's crumpet' is used to describe celebrities who have both brains and beauty, with Joan Bakewell being the most cited example. Generally, the term applies to a woman who looks like she may be willing to be a whore in the bedroom, an enthusiastic cook in the kitchen and a jolly useful addition to the pub quiz team.

CUCUMBER SANDWICHES

In aspirant middle-class circles, the cucumber sandwich is seen as the bread-based snack to be seen with when sipping afternoon tea on the lawn. It is a little known fact that the invention of this sandwich was actually down to mischievous minor royals out to prove that the middle classes would eat anything if they thought it would make them appear to be higher up the social scale than they actually are. Best eaten with the crusts removed, for added affectation.

CUSTARD

In fancy circles, such as the marketing meetings of ready-meal manufacturers for upmarket supermarkets, our beloved milky yellow pudding lubricant is known as crème anglaise, which makes it sound like some terrible Gallic euphemism for semen, perhaps in revenge for us calling condoms 'French letters'. Traditionally, custard was made from eggs, milk and cream, but everyone knows that the real thing is made from Birds custard powder or simply comes ready-made out of a tin. Our love for custard was highlighted by a news story in January 2008, in which banged-up bad boy Newcastle United footballer Joey Barton was reported to be warding off attacks from fellow prison inmates by buying them custard. After all, what hardened lag could resist its soothing yellowness? Custard powder is highly explosive in large quantities and can create a delightfully vanilla-scented explosion if not handled correctly. For this reason you are not encouraged to take your custard powder as hand luggage when you take your two-week package holiday in Spain and should instead stow it in the hold alongside your tea and Marmite.

DAFFODILS

This flower is often associated with the Welsh, as it can be worn on the lapel to celebrate St David's Day. But the bright yellow flower also serves to welcome in the spring and remind the whole of the UK that it is Mother's Day. Florists open early on Mothering Sunday to catch the trade as we go to visit parents, but tradition states that the correct gift for this day is daffodils that have been stolen from a public park, grass verge or, if all the free daffs have gone, bought from a petrol station forecourt.

DARWIN, CHARLES

From relative obscurity in the field of geology, Shropshire-born Darwin rose to be one of the most unpopular men of all time, so we are naturally proud that he is one of us. The disdain and even outright hatred for Darwin grew from his 1859 book *The Origin of Species* and other progressive works, which have long been used as a benchmark in disproving the existence of God, as well as putting forward the idea that we may have evolved from other primates.

Some see his worst crime as perpetuating the career of the ever so slightly creepy Richard Dawkins, whose books, such as his recent *Tooth Fairy: All Lies,* regularly top the bestseller lists.

DECKCHAIRS

Now, let us get this straight: deckchairs are not all that difficult to put up. From 1945 to 1962 an estimated 65 per cent of British comedy was based on the concept of deckchairs being hard to assemble. Not a lot of funny stuff was happening during this period, obviously. What is more revealing about the deckchair is its design, in that it is very much about a slight lying back but not really about lying down. This is because we see lying down as being a sign of continental laziness, suspicious shiftlessness and loose morals. We may be on a day or week off by the sea, but we don't want to be seen as slovenly. What the deckchair says is that we want to sit almost upright and possibly listen to a man playing an organ on the pier (*see* PIERS). Sunloungers are very much something to argue with Germans over when overseas.

DEEP-FRYING

I once ordered a dish in a Chinese restaurant in California and my local friend said: 'You do know that is deep fried, don't you?' His tone of voice would not have been much different if he was informing me that my choice of dinner was made from fresh babies and cooked by a team of sex

offenders who used their fetid drool as a marinade. He did not realise that in the UK the words 'deep-fried' are seen more as a term of culinary reassurance than as a threat to health. We know that it means that whatever we are about to eat has been encased in some kind of batter or coating and then cooked at mind-numbingly high temperatures (*see* FISH AND CHIPS). This means that it will probably be free of most viruses and will also probably at least taste of something, even if it is only four-month-old cooking oil. The logical extension of our love of deep-frying has been the invention of the deep-fried Mars Bar – a batter soaked hot chocolate treat – and the deep-fried kebab. These dishes are mostly found in Scotland, where even salad is often deep-fried, as are soft drinks, schoolbooks and most furniture.

DICKENS, CHARLES

The author of *A Christmas Carol* and *Nicholas Nickleby* is much admired for his portrayals of life among the lower orders in the Victorian era, though not so much admired for his rather dull visitor attraction in one corner of a discount shopping mall in Chatham's former naval docks. But Dickens is remembered more for the contribution that his own name has made to the language than for his literary efforts, with the term 'Dickensian' summing up any amount of poverty-induced squalor or unsafe working conditions. Contrary to popular belief, Dickens did not write *Oliver Twist* as a musical, though that is the version that everyone

both remembers and prefers, which does beg the question as to why its composer Lionel Bart does not have his own theme park and annual festival. The numerous Dickens-themed festivals and events around the country attract a large number of Britons who like to dress up in period costume, though pox-ridden whore, gin-addled mother of eight and hunchbacked child chimney sweep are not among the more popular modes of fancy dress, which mostly feature bonnets.

DINING AT THE ROADSIDE

As you travel around Britain's roads you will realise that many of us find it hard to get from town to town without the need to stop off for a warm snack and a mug of strong tea. Roadside catering vans dot the A-roads of Britain, offering the difficult choice between a sausage sandwich and a bacon sandwich, as well as between both colours of sauce (*see* HP SAUCE). Oddly, Indian or Chinese food has not taken off in these vans, with the same kind of all-day breakfast cuisine also being offered in our motorway cafés, such as the ubiquitous Little Chef restaurants. These outlets differ from the roadside vans by offering indoor seating as well as staff that are obliged to wash their hands occasionally and who do not use the grass verge as a lava-tory. That said, I personally think that the food offered from a converted portable toilet by those growing potatoes under each of their seven fingernails is still preferable to most dishes that Little Chef serve up.

DOCTOR WHO

Born out of the British love of science fiction writers such as H G Wells, *Doctor Who* slowly grew from a scary vision of future time travel and galaxies beyond the stars to a rather camp interplanetary pantomime (*see* PANTOMIME) as the hopes of British domination of space exploration faded. The dandyism of John Pertwee's Who signalled the way in the early 1970s, but it was Tom Baker's interpretation that marked the time lord as a figure of eccentric fun. But shaky sets and silly scarves aside, the programme became internationally adored and respected, maintaining its family-friendly scares and good writing. The show's recent revival has shown that it is a winning formula, with the dashing eccentric doctor/sexy young female assistant set-up making sure that the whole family can sit down to watch, unlike when Sylvester McCoy was Doctor and everyone started to wish the Daleks would just win and get it all over with.

DOGGING

It perhaps says a great deal about us that one of our most recently celebrated sexual deviancies involves standing around in a car park watching other people have sex. This may seem odd, but look how much we like being close to our cars. Just visit any beauty spot in the UK and you will find a family having a picnic next to their car, with their backs resolutely turned on the beauty spot in a silent protest against its showiness. Dogging at once celebrates

our love of amateurism alongside our reputation for ambivalence about the sexual act itself. Thus, we wind up watching a middle-aged couple go at it on the back seat of their Mondeo whilst thinking: 'Well, I could join in, but then I would get messy and anyway these pants are clean on. Ooh, what shall I have for tea? I like that car blanket they are doing it on'.

DOGS

Whether we are walking our King Charles spaniel, petting our poodle or pitting our illegal pit bull against a friend's Staffordshire bull terrier in a pub basement, we credit Man's Best Friend with feeling affection back and with probably more intelligence than we would a snarling, slobbering human who we had to clean up after each time they went to the toilet. Recent incidents of dogs attacking children have lead to further campaigns by some groups of dog lovers to blame owners and individual dogs rather than certain breeds for these problems, despite the fact that incidences of savage chihuahuas tearing the arms from infants have remained at a constant zero. Dog owners usually see cats as distant and spiteful, suitable only for crazy old ladies and lesbian couples who don't own a turkey baster. Greyhound racing is still a popular form of entertainment in Britain, with courses around the country attracting wannabe gangsters, gambling addicts and the kind of men who find the idea of dog breeding more stimulating than is healthy.

DOG POO

We are famous for being a nation of animal lovers, though we are sadly not so well known for being a nation that shows concern for what comes out of their rear end. This means that the pavements, parks and pathways of Britain are usually covered in dog poo. Treading in canine excrement is, apparently, lucky, though this is probably just some kind of odd pro-turd propaganda put about by lazy, irresponsible dog owners. Up until the 1980s white dog poo was just as common as the brown stuff, which was due to a now-abandoned government experiment. In the experiment some dog foods had phosphorent particles added, which would then aid dog-poo visibility. Scientists at the government-run Porton Down research centre wanted to go further, producing yellow crap that would glow in the dark, but cost-cutting measures put paid to these plans. Others claim that the white crap was down to ash and other fillers being put in the dog food, but that is just crazy talk.

DOLE

Until fairly recently, this payment was seen by many as the working-class equivalent of the gap year. The collection of unemployment benefit, income support or supplementary benefits was seen as a rite of passage by any teenager who did not really fancy (or could not gain entry to) work or university and who wanted to be a writer, musician, dreamer or waster. In high-unemployment Britain in the 1980s and 1990s young people could quite easily take a year

out without anyone in authority expecting them to do anything as silly as get a job. After all, they may be trying for a baby and that takes time and dedication, especially if you are trying with two or three different potential mothers or fathers. The name dole comes from the handouts (or 'doling out') that were given to the needy, especially that which came from the church or from wealthy philanthropists. Some dole traditions of this kind still take place at certain times of the year around the UK, especially at Easter.

DONKEYS

These beasts of burden can often be seen working on farms in southern Europe, but only in Britain do we use them to ferry children up and down sandy beaches. First introduced at Margate, the donkey ride has become as much a part of seaside holidays as sandcastles, sunburn and being swept out into the shipping channel on a lilo. Their favourite food is ice cream and EU employment laws state that they must be paid the equivalent of one 99 (single flake) per week. No seaside postcard is complete without a picture of a donkey on it.

DOUBLE-DECKERS

London has always been famous across the globe for its red double-decker buses, but these are also a part of life around the whole of the UK. Not only can they carry lots of people efficiently, but they also provide a neat guide to your place in life and in society. As a teenager the only place you should be sitting is at the top and at the back. This allows you to try

out all the ring tones on your mobile phone while you draw graffiti on the back of the seats and glower at other passengers. As you move into your twenties and thirties you will slowly move forwards, toward the safety of the stairs and an easy escape route in case anyone should start to look at you a bit funny. The only exception to this rule is the front seat on the driver's side, where anyone of any age can take a turn at pretending to be a bus driver, or just stare down the periscope at the driver's bald patch. From the age of 40 onwards you should sit downstairs and contemplate life's complexities while listening to your iPod and reassuring yourself you are still quite hip. Beyond that you move forward towards priority seating, tutting when no one gives up their seat for you and glaring at young mothers when they try to get on with a pram.

DOUBLE ENTENDRE

A central plank of British comedy for many years, this French phrase describes the wonderfully inventive ways that comics can play with our language using double meanings. The form came to light in slang and in acts in the theatres and music halls, so as to befuddle the upper classes and the censors. It was even thrown into acts to make the audience feel they were part of this conspiracy to get away with something, where adult themes were hidden in seemingly innocent sketches or songs. So, *She Sits Among the Cabbages and Peas* could be an innocent tale about a young girl lazing around in some vegetables or a dirty ditty about urination.

The filth is in your own mind, which makes it all the more amusing. The 1970s saw a double entendre boom, with the *Carry On* series of films (*see* CARRY ON), *The Two Ronnies* and *Are You Being Served?*, where shock-haired Mrs Slocombe would talk endlessly about her pussy and how it got damp the previous evening. *James Bond* films (*see* BOND, JAMES) carried a similar level of sexual double entendre, with the character Pussy Galore being one glaring example.

DRAG

The act of men dressing up as women is a complex part of our culture that has a huge number of unspoken rules and just as many apparent contradictions. Drag can be a cosy part of our family entertainment, evening comedy shows or even Sunday lunchtime pub singalong, but as soon as the man dressing as a woman actually tries to look like a woman and not a pantomime dame then a line is crossed. This is mostly because many British men know their propensity to go for a drunken grope of anything that looks vaguely female and do not want to have to check what sex the object of their lust is before advancing.

DR MARTENS BOOTS

Are you sitting down? Good. Then I have some shocking news to impart. This most British of boots – which has served the police, postmen and members of Combat 18 since the 1960s – is actually a German invention. Invented by a Doctor Maertens to help with a foot injury he had, the

famous air soles of the boots were first made from rubber left behind in Luftwaffe airfields after World War II. The idea was imported and the name anglicised in 1960, with the famous 1460 boot taking its name from the date of its release, 1 April 1960. It became fashionable as street wear for skinheads and punks and has grown from being available in simply eight or ten holes and in black or cherry red to being available in all kinds of designs and colours. Of course, all of the other designs and colours are horrible and should only be worn if you are a teenager with an identity crisis on your way to Camden Market. The boot was celebrated in song by comedian Alexei Sayle, who was just one of the boot's celebrity fans. The boot was made in Britain until 2003, when the business moved its manufacturing base to China.

EASTENDERS

First written to be a BBC Schools programme (*see* THE BBC) that would act as a deterrent for teenagers who wanted to run away to the big city, *Eastenders* portrays London as a place where you will most likely wind up dead or married to one of a pair of diminutive skinhead brothers who love their mum almost as much as they love domestic violence. Citizens of the East End are forbidden to own washing machines, so social life centres around the local launderette, though it is closed on Wednesdays to deal solely with Pat Butcher's 'smalls'. Eastenders star Barbara Windsor is on standby to become head of state should Britain take a sudden turn towards republicanism.

ECCENTRICITY

Foreign visitors and observers from afar love to witness and comment on British eccentricity, which we take to be an endearing admiration of our eclecticism and propensity to be unusual. This is not what they are actually saying. What they mean is that Britain is essentially a lunatic asylum

whose gates they enjoy rattling. If someone called you a nutter in a pub you would probably offer to settle the matter outside (perhaps proving their point), so it is our duty to take on the rest of the world until they are eating hospital food and not calling us mad anymore, or at least not to our faces.

ELGAR, EDWARD

Moustachioed nineteenth-century composer Edward Elgar wrote the *Pomp and Circumstance Marches*, from which *Land of Hope and Glory* was culled and has become an unofficial anthem for Britain. The song is used as the official anthem for England at the Commonwealth Games (*see* COMMONWEALTH) and draws upon Britain's naval heritage and our mastery of the seas. Elgar was seen as a deeply patriotic writer, though some of his more poetic works, such as *The Dream of Gerontius* would have been dismissed by the tabloid press as far too poncy and highbrow had they been written today. To be fair, though most music not created as a result of reality TV shows is seen as a bit poncy by most tabloids today. Elgar was a fan of Wolverhampton Wanderers Football Club who cycled to matches and even wrote a chant for their fans on one occasion based around the words 'We bang'd the leather for goal'. It didn't catch on, but *Land of Hope and Glory* can still be heard at nearly all football grounds in one of two variations, with fans using it as the backing tune to sing about their hatred for rival teams or their love of following their own team.

EMPIRE

It seems almost unbelievable now, but in the early twentieth century Britain effectively ruled one-quarter of the world population and one-quarter of the world's landmass. The Empire was expanded by our skill in trade and in seafaring, though bloodshed, robbery and slavery did play a large part as we went on to control vast swathes of Asia and Africa, as well as Australasia and parts of the Americas. Most of this was simply down to us looking for somewhere where we would not have to constantly remark, 'Ooh, isn't it parky this morning?' and our innate desire to get on the property ladder, somehow. All that is behind us now, with only a few rocky outcrops remaining and the Commonwealth surviving simply for those countries that like to see our Queen on their money or stamps. Of course, the Empire has also been a major source of immigration to the UK; mostly via offering those in former colonies some low-paid work by way of apology for generations of profiteering on their land. In exchange, we left the colonies with cricket, rugby (both of which they now beat us at) and an overwhelming amount of bureaucracy. In fact India became so efficient in the ways of British-style bureaucracy that we now outsource much of our paper pushing to Mumbai. We have also benefited from the arrival of un-bland food that immigrants brought with them, as well as from their cultural input. Canada has been a bit lax in contributing though, and has only offered the odd Bryan Adams CD.

THE ENGLISH CHANNEL

Yes, half of it may technically be the French Channel, but who really cares what they say or think about anything, apart from when you need to get there to buy some cheap booze and the lot of them are on strike. The 21 miles across the Channel have long been seen as a challenge by British swimmers, mostly because the arduous journey represents a chance to pick up some duty free fags and booze without having to pay for a ferry crossing. Channel swimmers famously smear themselves with grease before starting their crossing. Many use goose fat as insulation during their Channel swim, though when comedy actor and writer David Walliams undertook his swim he utilised fat that had been liposuctioned from several of his celebrity friends.

ERNIE

While the rest of the world was holding lotteries, rubbing off scratchcards and generally whooping it up by winning millions, we in Britain retained our composure and dignity by being happy with the unfussy act of being rewarded with £50 by an anthropomorphised random number generator. ERNIE, or Electronic Random Number Indicator Equipment as his close friends know him, has selected the Premium Bond numbers since 1957, bringing fleeting very minor elation to millions. The Premium Bonds are a peculiarly British form of gambling, where you can get your money back if you don't win, as you are essentially investing in a government bond where the dividend is the chance to

win a prize. The arrival of the National Lottery (*see* NATIONAL LOTTERY) made Premium Bonds seem about as sexy as thermal underwear, but they still remain a largely unspoken minority taste for conservative thrillseekers in much the same way as admiring Damart long johns does.

EXPLORATION

We Brits have always been renowned for pushing the boundaries of exploration, as we set forth from our tiny island in search of bigger, hotter, colder, wetter and drier places (*see* EMPIRE), as well as those requiring a level of mortgage less than six times our salary. This exploration lead to the acquisition of many of our colonies, as well as to the odd war or seven, often due to the fact that some darned foreigner claimed to have discovered the place first and because the natives did not speak enough English to really enable either side to resolve the matter amicably. Francis Drake, Walter Raleigh and James Cook are all celebrated seafaring explorers, but we hold a very special place in our hearts for those who have attempted to explore the Poles (the Polar regions that is, not those chaps from Krakow who renovated your bathroom). This fascination is largely down to the hardship faced by those trudging across the ice, leaving behind toes and bits of ear as they go. It also has a lot to do with our desire to find triumph in tragedy. Shackleton, Fiennes and Scott are all names that spring to mind when you speak of British explorers (though Shackleton was Anglo-Irish), but it is the contribution of

Captain Oates on Scott's polar expedition that we remember best, when he gallantly wandered off into the snow saying, 'I am just going outside and may be some time'.

FAGGOTS

Oh, how times change the meaning of a word, with this traditional West Midlands melange of pork offal declining in popularity ever since Hollywood brought us the derogatory American interpretation of the term (*see* HOMOSEXUALITY). Many men now baulk at the idea of cheerily informing their workmates that they are off into town to pick up some faggots, though some do use this confusion as an excuse to their wives when arrested for offering sexual favours to an undercover police officer at a local public convenience. The main UK manufacturer of faggots is Brain's, which doesn't really get the product off on the right foot and lets your mind wander too far from offal. In 2003, Brain's tried to re-popularise their product by starting a nationwide search for a 'faggot family' to head up its National Faggot Week campaign. Our transatlantic cousins found it hard to contain their mirth at the whole concept when it was reported online and on news channels, especially when the names of the winners were announced: the Doody family.

FÊTES

Every summer, our rural communities (*see* VILLAGES) and school playgrounds are filled with the sounds of breaking crockery, smashing pianos and the retching of underage drinkers being sick on some Crème de Menthe that they won on the tombola. The summer fête is both a celebration of the amateur and an insight into the dubious hobbies and talents of those who live around us. So we can enjoy the food-poisoning lottery of various homemade chutneys and cakes as well as discover that our neighbour's spaniel is a dab hand at doggie gymkhana or that the local greengrocer breeds ferrets and can play almost all of the current top ten on the spoons. The highlight of any fête is always something with a competitive element, whether that is the piano smashing competition between local pubs, the *It's a Knockout* contest involving parents and teachers (*see* IT'S A KNOCKOUT) or simply the awarding of prizes for the finest giant vegetables.

FISH AND CHIPS

Our national snack food combines the essential food groups of protein, carbohydrate and grease into what has traditionally been an affordable staple. Now, though, with dwindling fish stocks and climate change, the meal is becoming more an expensive treat than a regular meal. The white fish (be it cod, haddock, rock salmon or skate) should be dipped in batter and fried as fiercely as the chips. Arguments rage over whether nut oils or lard are best,

though everyone agrees that if you are served thin French fry-style chips with your fish then you should legally be allowed to spit in the face of the vendor. Salt and vinegar is essential, though this is also an area of dispute: some chip shops serve malt vinegar, some serve white vinegar and others offer acetic acid, which is branded as 'non-brewed condiment'.

FIVE WORDS

In 2007, Prime Minister Gordon Brown was searching around for a slogan for Britain that would neatly sum up the nation in five words or so and could be used as something for everyone to get behind. In the 1970s there was the 'I'm Backing Britain' campaign, which used similar calls for patriotism to help Britain work itself out of economic strife. Bruce Forsyth even released a record calling on workers to toil for an extra hour for no pay. Nice one, Bruce. Obviously, 'We're British, Innit' would make an ideal slogan for Britain and it's snappy enough, though 'Closed Half-Day on Thursday' would also work. 'Bugger off Fritz' would be popular, as would 'Fuck the French', especially if painted on the White Cliffs of Dover large enough to be read from Calais. We could use this exercise to make ourselves seem far cooler than we are. 'We'll sleep when we're dead' makes us sound like rocking party animals and would look pretty good emblazoned on the Union Flag. Perhaps we are better off sticking with what we know best, so 'Fancy a Cuppa?' (*see* TEA) or 'Britain: Bring an Umbrella' would both be perfect.

FLASKS

Whether you are attending a picnic in June or a football match in January then a flask is an essential piece of kit for keeping your tea or your oxtail soup at the correct temperature. The most British of flasks is the tartan variety, possibly showing the odd dent from picnic frivolity past or from when you had to use it to defend yourself against a gang of Millwall fans at London Bridge station. The vacuum flask (often simply known by the brand name of Thermos) can also be used to keep cold drinks cold, but that would be a very un-British thing to do, with the possible exception of lemon squash on a very hot day (the front page of at least one major tabloid should be about the heat for this to be applicable).

FLORAL CLOCKS

The floral clock is a largely dying art form, which was usually tended by civic gardening teams (*see* GARDENING) in seaside towns. These flowery timepieces would be set on cliff tops or prominent roundabouts, with the full clock face made from a bright array of flowers and bedding plants. The most famous floral clock in the UK is the original blooming chronometer in Edinburgh, which has been around since 1903. The Edinburgh clock still keeps time, but many floral clocks around the UK no longer function, simply being correct twice a day and having no actual clock mechanism. Floral clocks are seen as outmoded now, with most of us having watches or mobile phones to tell us the time. Some experiments were made with digital floral clocks in the

1980s, though the form could be in with a chance of a comeback, as Scarborough Town Council seeks to make their resort the first to have a floral internet.

FOLK MUSIC

British folk music could be said to be a major influence in the history of modern music, with many of the songs from these shores wending their way across the Atlantic and, eventually, into the roots of American rock. Yet our folk music is generally derided, not least of all by ourselves. Irish and American folk are both celebrated and perfectly acceptable to play at a party, whereas ours would generally clear a room. This is a shame, as our legacy of song includes some of the most interesting, twisted and violent ditties known to man. Even Eminem or 50 Cent would blush at some of the material. Though the legacy of British folk has been tainted by the existence of horribly floral saccharine folk-pop acts like Steeleye Span and the popularity of *Scotland the Brave* as a digital watch alarm tune during the early 1980s. But for that, teenagers would be standing on street corners trying to work out a three-part harmony to a particularly beautiful number about incest, rape and murder.

FOOTBALL

The people's game, as it is often known, was actually developed and established at fancy schools and universities in the mid-nineteenth century, though it eventually found its audience and its enthusiasts among working class men.

The Football Association was founded in England in 1863 and some of those original founders still remain in charge of the English game, being kept alive in oxygen tents at Soho Square and occasionally suckling at the man-breasts of Brian Barwick. The world's first international game was in 1872, between England and Scotland, and the FA Cup was founded the same year. Games from Britain are now seen the world over, meaning that up to 65 per cent of the world's population dislike Robbie Savage intensely, while an estimated 40 per cent are totally disinterested in the league position of Wigan Athletic.

FOOTBALL PHONE-IN SHOWS

We are the nation that gave football to the world, meaning that we have had the longest to develop folklore, rivalries, passion and incoherent bile about the beautiful game. All of these things and more come to a head on the football phone-in radio (or even, somewhat perversely, TV) shows, which usually take place just after games have finished. Fans call in to express elation or to contemplate managerial changes and new tactical formations, sometimes from the precipices of tall buildings. Everything from slating players' wages to suggesting the manager utilise a fifteen-year-old youth team player is acceptable, as is questioning the parentage of referees and the perceived sexual practices of rival teams' players. If possible, disputes from games in the early 1900s should be dragged up and used to rubbish opponents' ethics, playing style or choice of shirt design.

FOOTBALL POOLS

This system of guessing the outcome of various football matches has always been seen as the working man's way of escaping his lot and striking it rich, enabling him to stick two fingers up to the boss and buy a villa in Spain. Started by Littlewoods in 1923, the predicting of draws or wins was seen as a skill rather than game of chance, placing it outside the existing gambling laws. Before long the prizes available ran into hundreds of thousands of pounds and then reached a million pounds. Gathering around the radio or television for the football results at 4.45 pm on a Saturday became an act of almost religious significance for huge swathes of the population. During the winter months a shadowy cabal known as the Pools Panel sit in darkened rooms to decide what they think the outcome of postponed matches would have been, so that the right number of points can be awarded to those who have predicted the game may have been a win or draw. No one knows who the members of the panel are, though recent rumours have included Elvis, Lord Lucan and Shergar, who is said to stamp once for a draw and twice for an away win.

FOX HUNTING

Mixing our propensity for caring about anything with a fluffy tail (*see* NATION OF ANIMAL LOVERS) with our natural urge to wage class war, the subject of fox hunting has been a political hot potato for over a hundred years. A ban on the bloodsport came into force in February 2005, with members

of the pro-hunting Countryside Alliance predicting that the countryside would become a barren wasteland without large groups of people in red coats riding around chasing after foxes. But it was all still there last time I looked, green fields and all. Many of the hunts have found ways of defying the ban, now having to be every bit as ingenious as those who used to campaign against and sabotage hunts. Perhaps the most marvellous part of the whole hunt ban end game was the surreal sight of thousands of tweed-clad toffs (*see* HARRIS TWEED) marching through the streets of London while crusty punks stood on the sidelines cheering on police brutality and pondering whether these people didn't have jobs to go to (with many being from the landed gentry they indeed did not have jobs to go to, unless you count their seat in the House of Lords).

FRIED BREAKFAST

Also known as the full breakfast and usually featuring the name of the part of Britain it is served in, this is the breakfast that tourists expect to be faced with when they visit the UK (*see* BED AND BREAKFAST). There are various arguments about what it should include, but bacon, sausage, fried eggs and some form of tomato seem to be agreed upon by all, with baked beans (*see* BAKED BEANS) being essential unless you are served it somewhere that fancies itself as upmarket. The full English can include fried bread and black ('blood') pudding, whereas the full Scottish can also feature white pudding and a slice of square

sausage. Welsh diners expect lava bread (a mix of oats and seaweed) before their breakfast can be considered 'full', and an Ulster fry must contain a slice or two of the soda bread, known as farl, before it is complete. A full breakfast should feature tea and toast and be followed by ten hours of punishing physical labour or a two-hour lie-down. Overseas visitors should not attempt to complete the breakfast ritual on successive days without training their stomach for at least two weeks before their trip to the UK by swallowing at least a kilo of bread soaked in animal fat each day.

FRIED CHICKEN

In the beginning we only had Kentucky Fried Chicken in the UK, with their creepy Colonel Sanders, their bargain buckets and their secret blend of herbs and spices. Being Brits, we grew tired of this chickenopoly and so imitations began to spring up in every town centre, meaning that the streets became ankle deep in chicken bones and our high streets ever more emblazoned with the stars and stripes of the USA. Naturally none of these shops could claim to be making fried chicken that hailed from Kentucky, so they instead invoked the name of any vaguely southern-sounding state or just added something folksy to the word 'chicken', so we wound up with Dixy Chicken and the fantastically poorly-judged Chicken Cottage. Presumably no one has told them that the name of their restaurants make them sound like a public toilet where one might go to pick up young boys. Oh, come on! People are sniggering as they go past.

FRUITCAKE

The combination of dried fruits, nuts and spices into a cake makes for one of our nation's favourite accompaniments to tea and provides a truly evocative taste of Britain. Whether soaked in whisky, smothered in Christmas icing or made eggless in wartime, the fruitcake is a staple that we do not like to go too long without. It is often the subject of a 'guess the weight of the cake' competition at village fêtes (*see* FÊTES) and has also sustained and cheered British troops in battle. The cake also gives us just one of the many British names for the eccentrics that make up our populace, with a fruitcake being shorthand for a lovable-yet-unhinged individual. It is a little known fact that the Queen is a dab hand at making fruitcake and enters her efforts into the baking competition at a local fête, using a pseudonym. Her Dundee cake won second prize last year, though her standard fruitcake was unplaced.

FUDGE

No matter where you go in the UK you will be able to walk into a shop in that town and buy a box of fudge with a picture postcard of where you are attached to the front. The fudge industry is now more important than coal mining, with many small towns now living on a fudge-based economy. This has been taken to its logical and almost terrifying conclusion in the New Forest town of Burley, where every retail outlet has now been turned over to the selling of fudge. This has lead to several problems in

the area, with those new to the area running out to the corner shop for milk only to return with a half-pound of rum and raisin-flavoured fudge. Similarly, the takeaway food options are somewhat unorthodox, with local byelaws dictating that The Peking restaurant can only offer Szechuan fudge or a very sweet and only slightly sour fudge dish.

GARDEN FENCES

A good garden fence is said to make for good neighbours. It should be large enough to stop them peering over whenever you are having a barbecue or when your teenage daughter is experimenting with topless sunbathing, but it should also be low enough so you can at least exchange a few words about the weather over it. Ownership and repair of fences can be a great source of trouble between neighbours, but you should remember that ownership in most cases is split right down the middle of the fence itself. You own the piece that is on your side of the property, so even if your neighbour had paid for it to be put up you still have the right to draw an oversized phallus on your side, accompanied by an arrow and the word 'wanker' (*see* WANKER). The growing of *Leylandii* trees as fencing caused a large number of neighbour disputes in Britain, with the fast-growing trees eventually tamed by the Anti-Social Behaviour Act of 2003 (*see* ASBO), which was a bit of a letdown for vindictive lonely types with green fingers.

GARDENING

The British love of gardening is reflected in our economy, our leisure activities and our television scheduling, with even the time away from digging and hoeing spent buying books to tell us how to do it better, travelling to garden centres or watching programmes about it. The garden is our gym, our therapist and our escape. Without begonias to pot on, leaves to mulch and slugs to kill we would probably be engaged in some kind of bloody civil war. The Radio 4 programme *Gardener's Question Time* is essential listening for anyone who wishes to understand our love of the pastime. The show shifts the subject of gardening up towards the intensity of fierce political debate, and there was even gossip about the formation of a breakaway provisional wing of the Royal Horticultural Society after a 1992 on-air disagreement between panellists about the correct pruning of fruit trees.

THE GERMANS

We shall fight them on the beaches (*see* CHURCHILL, WINSTON), we shall fight them on the football field and we shall fight them over the sunloungers. Everyone needs a nemesis and our longest-running, most deep-rooted animosity is definitely reserved for Germany and its people. Every sitcom has had its German victims (most notably in the 'Don't mention the war' skit in *Fawlty Towers*) and the tabloid press (*see* TABLOIDS) goes into anti-German overdrive when we come up against Fritz – I mean Germany – in

a football tournament. Names such as krauts, the Hun, the Bosch, squareheads and sauerkraut-munchers are bandied around and allusions to our victories in 'two World Wars and one World Cup' are made. This conflict goes back to World War I and beyond, though the uncomfortable truth may be that our hatred is largely due to a loathing of how closely we resemble our Teutonic cousins. They are, after all, the mainstream Europeans that white Britons most resemble physically, our cuisines are held in similar disdain and both sides of the British Royal Family have German ancestry. We fight them because we fear becoming them, with their efficient motor industry, much-admired economy and tendency to examine their stools of a morning.

GIN AND TONIC

This popular cocktail was invented in India by medics in the British Army, who had to find a way of making the anti-malarial drug quinine palatable to the troops. The tree bark extract, which is an ingredient of tonic water, is extremely bitter and the gin masked its flavour, as well as being alcohol. And what Brit doesn't like alcohol, eh? (*See* BINGE DRINKING.) Commercial tonic waters are now less bitter, as they contain less quinine and more sugar. Quinine has become outmoded as an anti-malarial, as scientific advances have unearthed more effective drugs. But no British pub would be complete without a bottle of London (or Plymouth) gin on show and a crate full of tonic bottles. Despite its army connections, gin and tonic

is most often considered to be a lady's drink, perhaps due to the associations with grimey 1960s 'kitchen sink' dramas where women from the north of England (usually played by Rita Tushingham) would drink a good deal of the stuff before having a hot gin bath in an attempt to effect a home abortion.

GLASTONBURY

This Somerset town, with its famous tor, is said to have been the seat of Arthurian legends as well as the site where Jesus may have walked upon England's green and pleasant land (in the hymn *Jerusalem*) (*see* JERUSALEM), though most of us know Glastonbury for its connection to the pop festival of the same name, which actually takes place at nearby Pilton on Michael Eavis's Worthy Farm. Originally a hardcore hippie event that was a benefit for the Campaign for Nuclear Disarmament and attended by those who had celebrated the Solstice at Stonehenge, Glastonbury Festival is now a symposium for current and future middle management types, where break-out rooms and opportunities for blue-sky thinking have replaced teepees and drinking mushroom tea to open your mind, though falafel is still the only food available. Each year the rest of the nation prays for rain and revels in the Somme-like conditions endured by those attending, noting that only a barrage from an array of field guns could make matters marginally more amusing.

GLYNDEBOURNE

Like the Glastonbury Festival without chins (*see* ARISTOCRACY), the Glyndebourne Festival Opera is a big seasonal musical celebration for those who consider Mahler to be ghastly pop music for young people with long hair and poor hygiene. Social status at Glastonbury may be established by who has the best drugs, but at Glyndebourne it is established by who has the richest father, the most expensive picnic blanket and how many servants it took to prepare or collect the picnic spread upon it. Tickets are allocated on a strict system of entitlement: members of the landed gentry are served first; those with a *Who's Who* entry second, and any tickets then left are made available to the hoi polloi.

GNOMES

The garden gnome is actually a German invention, but let's ignore that shall we? After all, we did finally let Prince Philip bring over his German relations for his Diamond wedding anniversary in 2007. The humble gnome, whether he is fishing, pushing a wheelbarrow or simply basking in the sun, has grown in popularity since his introduction in the mid-nineteenth century, and the garden ornaments now are a symbol of the British suburban garden. Frowned upon as unspeakably common by some gardeners, the gnome is often viewed as a rather crude decoration, which has not been helped by the introduction of mooning gnomes and even naked gnomes. Often the subject of

childish practical jokes, gnomes are one of the most frequently stolen items from British gardens, and are usually the victims of kidnap by shady groups like the Gnome Liberation Front or Middle-Aged Men With Too Much Time On Their Hands (as they are also known). Some say that garden gnomes do possess mystical powers, while others claim that it is very bad luck to smash up your neighbour's gnomes with a cricket bat, especially if they have CCTV in their garden.

GOLF

Thought to have originated in Scotland in the twelfth century, golf has been delaying Sunday lunch and annoying golf-sceptic spouses ever since. Traditionally a game of the middle-aged and the middle class, a round of golf has long been seen as a place to secure business deals as well as to build a tolerance for brightly coloured trousers and Argyll jumpers. Between the ages of 42 and 60, 47 per cent of British men will buy a pair of red or yellow trousers from Marks and Spencer and wear them an average of once before realising how ridiculous they look. With its endless gadgetry and inbuilt snobbery, golf is the perfect game for the British man, affording plenty of opportunities for one-upmanship, a crafty drink and time away from the wife. Golf is played over 18 holes, though most golfers will tell you that their favourite hole is the 19th: this is how the bar at the end of the course is referred to. No matter how many times they repeat this, golfers will always think that this

piece of information is far more amusing than it actually is. If you are particularly snooty then you will pronounce golf as 'goff', which makes it sound like a game for depressed 15-year-olds who like cider and black clothes, ignoring the fact that the pale-faced teens would be scared off by the potential for exercise and the prevalence of polo shirts in the clubhouse.

GOSSIP

Whether it is over the garden fence, in the pages of magazines like *Heat*, *Now* and *Closer* or on websites like Popbitch and Holy Moly, we simply cannot get enough gossip in the UK. The newspapers employ columnists to keep us updated on political and pop gossip, while a wicked whisper about an un-named celebrity can bring offices to a halt until the name of the miscreant has reached everyone by email. We even have mini-skirted slatterns going out of their way to sleep with celebrities purely so that they can 'shag and brag' in the tabloid press for a cash payout. You might think that celebrities would grow tired of this kind of coverage, but many now employ publicity companies to make sure that their cellulite gets a decent page position and that their sexual peccadilloes make the front pages. Some celebrities even cultivate gossip-worthy stories to keep them in the pages of the press, and plastic surgeons are now seeing a growing demand for operations to add cellulite, as that usually gets more coverage than weight loss or a breast enlargement. Various celebrities, who I

cannot name, are rumoured to have discussed having facial warts grafted on or an arm amputated in order to get front-page coverage from *Heat*.

GRAMMAR
In some parts of the UK, grammar is the woman who is married to your grandfather, but in recent years we have begun to once again appreciate the beauty of our language, thanks largely to the slew of books and TV programmes on the subject. As a rule, we don't bother with all that masculine/feminine stuff that so blights other languages and makes them hard to learn, but we do have standards, and even dedicate some of our schools solely to the pursuit of good grammar. These schools are largely located in areas politically dominated by the Conservative Party whose members have impeccable manners and faultless grammar, which usually comes in handy when explaining away a mistress or making a commitment to social housing while trying to maintain a straight face. Novelist and columnist Tony Parsons once described Britain's grammar schools as 'public schools without the sodomy'.

GRAND NATIONAL
This jump race is the biggest horse race in the UK calendar and attracts more office sweepstakes, one-time bets and comment than any other race. Only the Derby comes close in terms of interest, but there is something about the combination of the huge field of runners, the arduous course and the

risk of injury or death to both horse and rider that appeals to our love of animals, sport and carnage. The race, which is held at Aintree, is run over a distance of just over four miles, with challenging fences such as the Chair, Becher's Brook and the Canal Turn all being familiar names to most Brits. Rules of the Grand National state that anyone watching at home is allowed to slap any member of the family who asks why the horses with no riders aren't allowed to win the race.

GREASY SPOONS

That one of Britain's culinary institutions is named after some badly-washed cutlery will probably come of no surprise to any foreign visitors who have accidentally wandered in to these temples to coronary heart disease. Famed for their vast all-day breakfasts (*see* FRIED BREAKFAST), fast turn-around and industrial strength tea, these cafés keep the building trade and white van man topped up with just enough saturated fat to keep them going without them keeling over clutching their chest until the job is done. This is a very subtle and difficult balance to maintain, with skilled greasy spoon artisans honing their arts over a lengthy career at the hotplate. They should be able to simultaneously fry six eggs, pour a dozen teas (with three sugars each), tot up a bill, give out some racing tips and read the *Sun*. Greasy spoon coffee is deliberately kept undrinkable. This serves the purpose of keeping out the middle classes and gangs of yummy mummies with buggies as well as ensuring that painters and plasterers don't get all jittery by mid-afternoon.

GREAT BRITAIN

In Britain we have a confusion of names that we can refer to when someone asks where we come from. We could say England, Scotland, Wales or Northern Ireland, we could say the United Kingdom or we could even say the United Kingdom of Great Britain and Northern Ireland. But by far the best answer to give is Great Britain. Historians suggest that the name comes from a description of the main landmass of Britain, which ignores the smaller islands and Northern Ireland. But the name is so obviously a superlative about how fantastic we all are and has been accepted by the rest of the world as just that. Other countries did consider adding descriptive terms to their names, but no one could really agree on the right prefix. The French were not happy with 'Garlicky' and Germany didn't like that fact that its near neighbours suggested both 'Likely to Start a War' and 'Excrement-Obsessed' to describe the nation. Likewise, Belgium didn't like the disdain implied in the name 'Probably Belgium'.

GREEN FIELDS

The green areas that surround our towns and which make up our countryside are an important factor in our national identity. We see ourselves as a green and pleasant land and identify with images of rolling hills, the jagged matrix of farmland and the hedgerows that surround them. Without our green fields there would be nowhere for builders to dump rubble and old kitchen suites, for huntsmen to flush out a fox (*see* FOX HUNTING), or for Tesco to eye up as

potential superstore sites. Rumours that the EU was planning to turn all of our fields brown and fill them with Polish immigrants were recently found to be untrue and possibly due to *Daily Mail* columnist Richard Littlejohn drinking too much coffee and then randomly hitting his computer keyboard with his car keys.

GUY FAWKES NIGHT

This jolly annual celebration of putting Catholics to death takes place on the 5 November each year, marking the foiling of a plot to blow up the Houses of Parliament in 1605. The plotters, for whom Fawkes was the explosives expert, planned to kill King James I by igniting gunpowder under the House of Lords at the state opening of Parliament. The gang was caught in the nick of time and then tortured before being tried and then hung, drawn and quartered. Children at school are taught a rhyme that implores them to 'remember, remember the fifth of November', though most schools don't carry on to the verse that talks about setting fire to the Pope after first choking him. An effigy of Fawkes is usually burnt atop a bonfire (the night is often called Bonfire Night), though anything from an effigy of the Pope to contemporary political figures is seen as acceptable in some parts of the UK. Fireworks are also let off for Guy Fawkes Night and these are traditionally ignited at 3 am on a council estate about three days before the big day.

HACKNEY CARRIAGE

These icons of the British taxi trade are mostly associated with London, but the black cab, as the design is sometimes generically referred to, is also used in other major cities in the UK. Since the advent of advertising on taxis, black cabs are not always black any more and the shape is changing as new designs come in, but the basic model is what makes them so well recognised across the world. They have a high roof and usually have space for five passengers, with three seats across the back and two pull-down seats that have their back to the driver. They are famed for being able to turn in the tightest of situations and are favoured by private enthusiasts as well as cab drivers; Prince Philip and Stephen Fry are both reported to be owners. In Britain, the Hackney carriage has the right of way over all other forms of transport, including cyclists, police cars, mothers pushing prams and old ladies on mobility scooters. A Hackney carriage driver will legally invoke his right of way by leaning out of the window and shouting 'Getofftheroadyoufuckingidiot', which is a traditional

phrase thought to date back to the days when the Hackney carriage was a carriage pulled by a horse.

HAGGIS

This mixture of sheep innards, boiled up in the animal's stomach with onion, oats, spices and herbs, is the dish that Scotland is most famous for. It is the subject of a famous poem by Robert Burns (*see* BURNS, ROBERT) and is served as the centrepiece of Burns' Night with a portion of 'neeps and tatties', which is mashed swede and potatoes. Naturally, the offal-based treat is also available deep-fried in Scotland's many chip shops and is just the kind of thing to settle your stomach after a night out on the booze. The strange shape and texture of the haggis has lead to much hoaxing over the years, with gullible tourists often being tricked into believing that the haggis is a wild animal that is hunted in the Highlands. The haggis is also possibly the strangest food to have been mimicked in a vegetarian version, which is made by famed haggis manufacturer MacSween. A spokesmen for MacSween commented that it would be an 'offal shame' if veggies didn't get to eat haggis on Burns' Night, or at least that is what I hope they would say. It is, after all, always a shame to miss out on such a fine opportunity for a pun: something that we Brits are renowned for. The origins of the name and recipe of haggis are somewhat of a mystery, with speculation placing its origins as far apart as Iceland (the country, not the super-market of the same name) and Rome.

HALF DAY CLOSING

Almost unthinkable today in our modern 24/7 cities, the tradition of half day closing is still adhered to in some smaller towns and villages. Usually falling on a Tuesday, Wednesday or Thursday, half day closing traditionally served to provide shopkeepers and shop workers with a break to compensate for working at the weekend. That this tradition still continues in a random assortment of locations is often of huge confusion to tourists, who turn up at 2.30 pm on a Thursday to buy some bread and are met with a ghost town. The towns and villages that still have half day closing are usually those where witchcraft and ritual sacrifice are still rife, with the half day being used to complete tasks associated with these practices, such as rounding up virgins and sharpening knives.

HARRODS

Founded in 1834, Harrods has risen from humble shop to major tourist attraction, with a trip to the enormous department store being right up there with a visit to Buckingham Palace or a ride on the London Eye for visitors to London. Acquired by the outspoken Mohammed Al Fayed in 1985, the store and its owner have seldom been out of the news since, especially since the death of Al Fayed's son alongside Princess Diana (*see* PRINCESS DIANA) in Paris in 1997. These deaths inspired Al Fayed to install what is perhaps the world's tackiest memorial, which can be winced at from outer space. Harrods is most celebrated for its luxury goods and has become a desirable brand in its

own right, with a Harrods carrier bag inferring that its owner may well be worth mugging, though nine times out of ten robbers will find that their victim is simply someone from the provinces who just bought a pair of socks to get a Harrods carrier bag.

HARRIS TWEED

You may think that the islanders of Harris, Uist, Barra and Lewis are taking the piss with the cost of their unique fabric, which is made from the wool of local sheep and finished by hand in the islanders' homes. But you should be grateful, as the islanders used to *give* the piss as well, with Harris Tweed previously being softened by a good soaking in local urine. The cloth is still favoured by the horsey set and the landed gentry, but its popularity in a previous era meant that the upper crust smelled of stale urine on a damp morning. Urine may no longer be a part of the process, but the cloth is still made using traditional craft methods on the Scottish islands, which sit between the Highlands in the Outer Hebrides. 'Tweedy' is still used to denote someone who is a little staid, stuck up and of the upper class, though Girls Aloud singer Cheryl Tweedy is none of the above. 'Tweed' is also the name of a perfume by Lentheric, usually brought by middle-aged salesmen for their disappointed mistresses. They would probably be more disappointed to receive Tramp, made by the same manufacturer. Nothing says 'I can't decide whether you smell like a homeless person or simply remind me of a whore' than a gift of Tramp.

HAVING A GO

The spirit of amateurism is alive inside most Britons, meaning we are willing to have a go at things even if we turn out to not be very good at them. Hence our joy in watching Eddie 'The Eagle' Edwards and his exploits in the world of ski-jumping as well as Boris Johnson and his efforts in forming a sentence without offending one or other section of the populace. But the term also refers to our intervention in matters of law and order, with the 'have-a-go hero' moniker often used to refer to extremely dead members of the public who decided to tackle masked gunmen raiding an armoured security van. Those who survive the having-a-go process are lauded in the press, with one recent example being Glaswegian baggage handler John Smeaton, who gave a sound thumping to a burning terrorist who had tried to blow up Glasgow Airport. 'If you come to Glasgow we'll set about you,' said Smeaton to the terrorists, repeating what had been the city's official tourist slogan until 1986.

HEDGEROW

Conceived as a natural way to break up land and protect crops from the wind, the British hedgerow has become a haven for wildlife and the source of some of our favourite fruits. No summer would be complete without some free blackberries picked in the countryside and winter would seem longer were there not sloe gin to sip by the fireside. Being natural, the hedgerow gives a soft edge to fields, and

allows the countryside to be seen as a continuous green mass when viewed from above. They are also used for the ancient rural equivalent of computer file sharing, whereby pornographic magazines are placed in hedges so that others passing by may also enjoy last month's copy of *Knave*.

HOLIDAY CAMPS
With the advent of paid holidays and the need for some serious leisure time after World War II, there was a boom in the nascent holiday camp industry, with Butlins and Pontin's holiday camps taking the majority of the business. Like giant council estates by the sea, these purpose-built resorts catered mostly for the working classes, providing cheap food, family entertainment and nylon sheets. They often traded on socialist-sounding slogans to create an image of holiday utopia where all were equally entitled to ogle bathing beauties. They also managed to make men proud of their knobbly knees and make those who had recently been prisoners of war feel like having fun in an environment that featured crowded accommodation and a perimeter fence. The holiday camp suffered when cheap foreign package holidays became popular, but they still cater for those on a tight budget. By contrast, the more modern and far costlier Centerparcs pretend not to be holiday camps, as they cater for the middle classes, who prefer a sun-blushed tomato to a tinned one. To me at least, Centerparcs simply feels like a Pontins with the addition of a wine list and a lack of karaoke.

HOME INTERNATIONALS

Nothing was such a large test of the bonds of the British nation as the Home Internationals, which was something akin to a civil war with referees and linesmen that took place annually from 1894 to 1984. A four-way football tournament between England, Northern Ireland, Scotland and Wales, the Home International Championships were a source of much rivalry, heavy drinking and fighting. Often overshadowed by larger competitions, such as the World Cup, the Home Internationals began a steep decline in 1977 when crowd trouble marred Scotland's 2-1 victory over England at Wembley. Scots fans famously broke the crossbar of one goal and dug up parts of the pitch to take home as souvenirs. A pitch invasion also marked the moment that Scotland 'became world champions' defeating then actual world champions England 3-2 at Wembley. Northern Ireland is current holder of the championship title, having won the tournament in 1984. It has not been played since, as hooliganism and the troubles in Northern Ireland made it increasingly difficult to hold games safely and without incident.

HOMOSEXUALITY

It may have been illegal up until 1967 (in England and Wales, 1980 in Scotland and 1982 in Northern Ireland), but we in Britain have always had something of a liberal attitude to homosexuality, just so long as it is confined to those who work in the arts. After all, how would theatrical costumes be

made and musical theatres financed were it not for gay men? And what would purveyors of sensible footwear do were it not for the lesbian market? Usually we have been accepting of overly camp grotesques such as Kenneth Williams (*see* CARRY ON), but homophobia is still prevalent in largely male environments, especially in sports where crowd and players alike could not countenance the idea of an openly gay Premiership footballer. Homosexuality is now tolerated in the armed forces, though it was not so in the days of Field Marshal Montgomery, who said: 'I have heard some say homosexual practices are allowed in France. We are not French... We are British – thank God!' Though Monty did fail to mention that he might have been at least a little 'bi-curious', as they say in the personal ads.

HOODIES

These current folk devils have taken the place of scary youth cults of yore such as skinheads, Teddy boys and rockers. Hoodies are responsible for approximately 92 per cent of crime in Britain, with offences such as looking a bit suspicious, being quite warm and giving the finger to David Cameron topping the list of regular hoodie outrages. Scientists have discovered traces of evil chemicals in almost all of the ordinary high street-purchased hooded sweatshirts that they tested, proving that these garments have the potential to turn the most mild-mannered teenager into a granny-slashing tearaway. In 2006 a group of elderly men and women started to wear hoodies in an attempt to make

them appear uncool and scare teenagers off wearing them, though they simply discovered that they were more susceptible to mugging from proper hoodies, as their own hoods lessened their peripheral vision.

HORNBIES

This term of abuse for middle-class (*see* CLASS) fans of Arsenal Football Club has spread to become a catch-all phrase for Johnny-Come-Lately followers of the game who sit meekly in expensive seats and were not around when their team was performing badly ('Where were you when you were shit?' being one the chants aimed at Hornbies and other glory hunters). The name derives from that of author Nick Hornby, whose memoir *Fever Pitch* spoke of his love for his team, though fans of Arsenal and rival clubs have pointed out that his devotion did not extend to actually travelling to the away game at Liverpool where Arsenal secured the 1989 league title. Such behaviour may now be described as Hornby-ish or Hornby-ite. His enthusiasm for the game and the success of *Fever Pitch* made football seem safe for the middle classes and also coincided with the abolition of the standing terraced areas, as well as the growth of corporate hospitality and executive boxes.

HORSE RACING

Known colloquially as the Sport of Kings, horse racing is actually a sport that defies class. There are divisions that define which race courses you may attend and what stand or

enclosure you may watch the race from, but it is enjoyed by everyone from the Queen to that scrotey-looking bloke who you regularly see at the newsagent buying a packet of Golden Virginia and a copy of *Escort* magazine. But you don't have to physically go to the races to enjoy them. Britain's streets are littered with bookmaker's shops, which show racing all day and where you can lose your money on ridiculous accumulator bets without leaving your neighbourhood. Unlike racing itself, the existence of a bookmaker in your neighbourhood does send a message about class. If they outnumber the coffee chains you live in a working-class area, if the reverse is true then you live in a middle-class area. If you have someone to make your coffee, place your bets and muck out your racehorses then you live in an upper-class neighbourhood.

HOUSE PRICES

The discussion of how much your home cost, when you bought it, how much equity you have and what the local schools are like is threatening to overtake the weather as the premier topic of conversation in the UK. In an ever-spiralling escalation, this conversation drives homeowner anxiety, which drives sales, which drives prices, which drives more conversation about houses. The huge amount of property porn on television does not help, with men being tricked into watching by generously proportioned double-fronted properties such as Kirsty Allsop and Sarah Beeny. Before they know what they are thinking they are suddenly upgrading to a three-bedroom cottage on the Fens with a *pied à terre* in

Northampton, even though they have lived in a one-bedroom flat in Belfast their whole life. Good schools with good reputations can make property prices rocket, so I try to keep prices low in my own neighbourhood by handing out baseball bats to local schoolchildren. I also steal their textbooks and kidnap the brightest ones when they are due to sit their GCSEs, thus artificially lowering the school's league-table position.

HP SAUCE

This brown, fruity, spiced sauce was always seen as the perfect accompaniment to a fried breakfast, with its label featuring the Palace of Westminster and its initials standing for Houses of Parliament. Produced in Aston, in the Midlands, HP Sauce sat with Heinz tomato ketchup at the top of the condiment tree until 2007, when its production (along with that of Heinz tomato ketchup) was moved to Elst in Holland. Upon hearing news of the switch many patriotic Brits decided to boycott the sauce, switching instead to the rival Daddies sauce, though this did seem to be out of annoyance at Europe in general rather than any particular siding with redundant workers. This boycott did not hit HP's manufacturers as hard as some may expect, as Daddies sauce is also produced by Heinz, in Holland. Rival brand Branston suggested that HP replace their picture of Parliament with one of a windmill, though some may prefer the image of Traitor's Gate.

ICELAND

In the recent past it was the trades unions or even the Labour Party that looked out for the working classes of Britain, but this duty has now fallen to frozen food chain Iceland, who provide golden brown food at affordable prices. From each according to their transfat content to each according to their need to have something with oven chips for tea (see TEA AS A MEAL). To signify this down-to-earth approach, the supermarket employs chesty celebrity mum Kerry Katona as their public face. Katona was selected for the role because she is the same colour as most of the food on sale in the store, though she also gives off the subliminal message that it may be best enjoyed pissed.

IMMIGRATION

This single word is the most likely to stir up controversy in Britain and always has been. When the Romans and the Vikings became immigrants to our shores they tended not to bother about passports, visas or hanging off the underside of a Eurostar train, and they were met with the same suspicion as

refugees or economic migrants are today. Rumours abounded that Vikings were being allowed to rape and pillage with impunity and even received central government funding to assist with some of the more difficult pillaging in outlying areas. Meanwhile, Romans were often spotted in the markets buying an excess of mead and driving the latest in chariots, which were rumoured to have been paid for out of social security cheques. In Britain, the question of immigration is mostly one of immediate concern. Our American cousins are proud to call themselves sixth-generation Irish or Italian, but after about two or three generations most immigrants become simply British, though sometimes retaining a suffix, such as British-Black or British-Asian. Oddly, these children of immigrants often have more sense of Britishness than those whose families have been here for generations, as these more established groups tend to divide into English, Scottish, Welsh or Irish. Racists are having trouble in recent years due to the sheer diversity of immigrants, thus leaving them unsure which race it is they currently dislike most, leading to embarrassing social difficulties when they want to abuse an individual.

IMPERIAL MEASUREMENTS
The 1970s saw the decimalisation of our currency and was also supposed to herald a switch over from miles to kilometres, pints to litres and fathoms to something more fathomable. But as a nation we stuck our fingers in our ears and went 'la, la, la, la, la, I can't hear you', so the problem went away for a while. Some metric measurements did start

to creep in, however, necessitating complex calculations by those in the building trade as they negotiated the problems of purchasing a metre of four-by-two or 250 cm of quarter-inch pipe. It was decided that changing speed limits to kph would probably cause accidents and that switching our pints of beer for litres would be similarly disastrous, as no man would want to be seen ordering a half-litre. EU regulations have seen the enforcement of metric weights and measures for the measurement of foodstuffs, but many market traders stood up against this imposition and this rebellion lead to the case of the so-called Metric Martyrs, who were deported to Australia in 2004. Other popular imperial measurements include the double-decker bus and the size of Wales. Wales is said to be the size of Wales, though no one has been able to measure it in double-decker buses as yet.

INNIT

This piece of punctuation can be used to end any sentence in Britain, providing a simple reaffirmation of the facts therein (It is well hot, innit?) or adding emphasis to the need for confirmation of a fact from a companion (Are you going to the cinema, innit?). The genius of the word, which is used in most sentences uttered by those still at school, is that it can be retrospectively applied to classic literature or speeches and still make sense. So, Shakespeare may ask 'To be, or not to be, innit?' while Churchill could have added emphasis with 'Never in the field of human conflict has so much been owed by so many to so few, innit?'.

INVENTORS

Innovators, inventors and engineers have always been a huge part of what has driven Britain on to success across the world (see EMPIRE). Without these single-minded individuals we would never have become the force we did in global business and politics. Without William Caxton's popularisation of printed works we would not have been at the apex of the literary world, without railway engineer and bridge builder Isambard Kingdom Brunel we would not have had the influence we did in infrastructure or the means to grow as an industrial nation, all of which was aided by Stephenson and his famed railway engines. Nowadays we look to the likes of James Dyson and clock-work radio inventor Trevor Bayliss to lead the way, though most of our inventors now find themselves being quizzed on TV business show *Dragons' Den*. Obviously Caxton would not have fared so well on the show himself, as it would have been a bit hard to get Theo Paphitis or Peter Jones to invest in printing when no one could actually read and not many books had been written for public consumption. In fact, female Dragon Deborah Meaden would have made him cry like a baby and would probably have given him a Chinese burn for good measure.

IRN BRU

Curing Scottish hangovers from primary school to nursing home, Irn Bru is the sticky-sweet beverage that claims to be made in Scotland from girders but is actually manufactured

by wringing out wasps that have settled in cans of Tizer (*see* TIZER). Like the super-expensive Kopi Luwak coffee beans that have been partially digested and excreted by small mammals, this process makes for a smoother, purer red fizzy pop. If you spot a Scotsman searching through the bins in your town centre it is highly likely that they are one of Irn Bru's highly skilled 'harvesters', whose job it is to track down the Tizery wasps.

IT'S A KNOCKOUT

It may have been adapted from a French television show, but this mix of obstacle courses and ridiculous outfits captured the hearts of our nation, and even leading to *It's a Royal Knockout* in 1987, where Princess Anne, Prince Andrew, Prince Edward and the Duchess of York took part in a celebrity-studded edition of the game. Pitting British town against British town, the contest sought to reveal whether the people of Slough were better than the people of Dundee or Dungannon when it came to carrying buckets of water while dressed as a giant and wearing outsized shoes. Whatever happened, host Stuart Hall would collapse with laughter, while co-host Eddie Waring would mutter something unintelligible. The show really came into its own in the international edition, when Minehead could be up against Munich and Marseilles. This truly became the peoples' Olympics, when a baker would compete with a builder and a doctor with a docker. Attempts have been made to bring the show back, but it was very much of it's

time, and peaked in 1973 when Britain's entry into the Common Market was decided in a special edition of the show that pitted Barnsley against Basel and Oslo.

JERUSALEM

This William Blake poem, set to music by Hubert Parry in 1916, is what many, especially those on the political right, would like to see as an English anthem (see NATIONAL ANTHEM). This is mainly because the verse sounds stirring, nationalistic and certainly more rousing than our current British dirge. The poem talks about the possibility that Jesus may have visited England, with the most likely site being Glastonbury in the years before the annual festival got all commercial and you had to be on the internet at the very moment that tickets went on sale. So far, so ridiculously unfounded you may think, but the main problem is the opening line of the poem. 'And did those feet in ancient time, walk upon England's mountains green?' it asks. The obvious answer is: 'No, now let's move on'. Things get trickier as the poem goes on, talking about not allowing your sword to sleep in your hand until we have built Jerusalem on a brown field site somewhere with good access to the M4. This is before we even get to the question of what Jerusalem should look like and if it should have affordable

housing as a condition of planning consent being granted. Obviously it would have a Tesco, Starbucks and drive-thru McDonalds, while the multiplex cinema would only show *Chariots Of Fire*.

JORDAN

The pneumatic model, whose real name is Katie Price, has been locked in a breast-size arms race with herself since she first appeared on the *Sun*'s Page 3 (*see* PAGE 3). Having augmentation surgery meant that she could no longer fulfil Page 3's 'natural only' policy, but her ever-swelling chest lead her on to a career that has seen her become one of the nation's best-known and highest-earning celebrities. Something of a constant contradiction, she often confounds and then confirms expectations of her. Her astute business decision to retain copyright over most photographs of her means that she even makes money when newspapers are slating her, though she didn't do herself many favours by standing for Parliament in 2001 on a platform for free plastic surgery for all, backed by the slogan 'for a bigger and betta future'. Jordan is now a bestselling author, which helps to fund her continuing surgery. Her recent breast reduction surgery upset the chiefs of English Heritage, who were preparing to slap a Grade II listing on the star's cleavage, reasoning that it is such a recognisable part of British Culture that it should be preserved in its prime. This would have meant that Jordan would have had to consult the preservation body before making any material alterations

and that Peter Andre would have to notify them in writing before gaining access to this site of national importance.

JUMBLE SALES

If you like fighting old ladies for urine-stained support hose then the jumble sale is the place for you. An institution of church halls and Saturday mornings, the jumble is an archetypally British affair wherein church volunteers will collect all the old clothes and toys that no one can be bothered to eBay and then put them in big piles to be sold off for pennies. Jumble sales attract mainly the elderly, though fashion students and antique collectors do attend on the off-chance of finding a Vivienne Westwood original or the odd Ming vase. Fleas, lice and moths are other favoured items that visitors take home with them.

KAGOULS

These waterproof coats are an essential for anyone planning a day out in Britain. Whether you own a £200 designer version or one that folds up into itself and comes from the Pound Shop, you should carry your kagoul with you on any walk or visit to a theme park or beach. Married couples in Britain are required by law to wear matching kagouls and these should be worn with matching jumpers if at all possible. Bridal kagouls are available for summer weddings and two-person models are available for the dogging community (*see* DOGGING).

KING HENRY V

Welsh-born Henry V was the most famously combative of monarchs and his portrayal in the Shakespeare play that bears his name has made this legend grow with time. It is his victory at Agincourt in 1415, which is portrayed in Shakespeare's play, that he is most celebrated for. It lead to his having control of France as well as England. He married Catherine of Valois in order to establish a lasting peace

between the two nations, but that didn't really work, did it? Still, he did come back with some decent duty free and some nice cheese. Henry V's rousing pre-battle speech from Shakespeare's play is often used to stir up patriotic pride or to inspire modern troops before battle.

KING HENRY VIII

As everyone who has ever studied British history knows, the sequence of the fate of Henry VIII's wives goes thus: divorced, beheaded, died, divorced, beheaded, survived. Not really a track record that would make him worth a punt if you saw his profile on an internet dating website, but a memorable record of adultery, killing and tragedy, even for a royal. Henry VIII, who is almost always pictured as a man of immense girth, was a dedicated sportsman in his youth, though he let himself go a bit when he got married, as many British men do. His waist was said to measure more than 50 inches when he died. The giant king was also responsible for the somewhat shady start of the Church of England, which was founded as a response to the Pope not allowing him to dissolve his marriage to Catherine of Aragon, who had failed to provide the king with a male heir. The King changed Britain to a Protestant nation and split with Rome, leading to the dissolution of the monasteries. The newly formed Church of England granted Henry VIII his divorce, kick-starting a record as the church that will agree to most things just so long as you turn up once every couple of years and help raise funds if someone nicks the lead off the roof.

KISSING

Continental visitors may be surprised to find that there are strict limits upon the number of kisses a Briton is entitled to dole out in one year. Because of these arcane restrictions we limit kissing on the lips to our partners and generally keep kissing on the cheek for grandmothers only. Those in the more artistic professions sometimes flaunt these restrictions by greeting all and sundry with a kiss on the cheek, but this is against the spirit of the law and also counter to the British way of life. It is sometimes acceptable for men to kiss women on the cheek, though only really when they fancy them and maybe try to slip mouthwards a little. It is also acceptable to kiss a friend's fiancé just to check that she doesn't have stubble and to get a close-in look at that suspicious Adam's apple. Hugging should be restricted to the sports field and only otherwise used in public when a friend has lost a loved one or their mobile phone.

KNOTTED HANDKERCHIEFS

Like the red squirrel, use of the knotted handkerchief as headgear has been all but killed off by an insidious American invader. In this instance I talk, of course, of that vile intruder the baseball cap, a sporting accoutrement for a sport we neither play nor understand in Britain. There was a time when no beach would be complete without rows of men protecting their balding pates by the swift application of a white handkerchief with a knot tied in each corner. This ad hoc millinery was a great example of British ingenuity,

and the traditional craft skill was passed down from father to son. It was imminently portable, good value and protected against both burning and skin cancer. Proud British men should start to reclaim this item of their headgear heritage. After all, if it was good enough for Monty Python and Alf Garnett then it is good enough for you.

KRAY TWINS
Had they been born in London's now-hip Hoxton just 50 years later than they were, the notorious gangster twins would probably have grown up to be web designers. But the Hoxton of 1933 was not the kind of place that men with fin haircuts, effete scarves, laptop bags and designer spectacles wandered about after dark. So the twins went on to run the criminal underworld of east London, committing murders along the way and collecting a surprising number of celebrity friends. Perhaps the oddest of these associates was bland TV newsreader, *How* panel member and game show host Fred Dineage, who became the pair's official biographer, ghost writing their memoirs. These memoirs gave rise to the 'geezer lit' genre, whereby anyone who had done much more than have a fight in the playground at school got to tell all about their toughness, crimes and loving their mum.

LANGUAGES

It is often said that but for the bravery of our forces in World War II we would all be speaking German by now. This is simply rubbish, because we are so poor at learning languages. We probably would have been able to ask for a beer by now, as well as chips (*see* CHIPS WITH), but there is no way we would be using ridiculously lengthy compound words or doing much more than just using English really loudly and slowly, as well as pointing at stuff and saying 'one...of...those'. Languages are taught in schools from an early age, but as we have a pathological hatred of most of the people whose languages we are learning we never seem to get that far. Most of us manage to take in that most French people are likely to be called either Jean-Paul or Claudette, but that is about the extent of our interest.

LAWNS

It is an unspoken rule in suburbia that your front lawn should be sufficiently well kept to host a game of test cricket (*see* CRICKET) should the need suddenly arise. Those who

stray from mowing their lawns each Sunday – employing heavy rollers, nail scissors and a small team of local Scouts to finish the job – are seen as social deviants and are unlikely be invited to the kind of event where everyone throws their car keys into a bowl at the end of an evening. The lawn should never be used for entertaining, sitting on or playing football on. It is there for bragging rights and social acceptance only and should not be seen as a leisure facility.

LEAVING THE COUNTRY

There is a long tradition of celebrity whingers claiming that they will leave Britain if X or Y were to happen. Traditionally these fits of attention-seeking pique are related to the potential election of a political party that has high taxation for moody celebrity whingers in its manifesto. The most famous recent example of this was when comedian Jim Davidson was one of many who said he would leave the UK if the Labour Party were elected to govern in 1997. It is thought that Davidson's promise directly influenced the landslide Labour victory, with turnout as high as 110 per cent in some areas of the country. Sadly Davidson didn't flee the country as soon as the results came in; instead he stayed behind to amuse the nation by becoming bankrupt. His failure to leave immediately has lead for calls for a declaration of 'I am off if...' to be legally binding. *Tubular Bells* composer Mike Oldfield threw a hissy fit of his own in 2007, in which he claimed his

leaving was due to the imposition of the ban on smoking in public places, though it was later revealed his exit was actually down to his being a twat.

LIMOUSINES

In many countries the stretch limousine is the vehicle of choice for heads of state or movie stars, but in the UK we have democratised this form of transport to the extent that it is now the taxi of choice for binge drinkers. The length of a limousine is always inversely proportional to the IQs of those travelling within it. For those who travel in limousines I should explain that this means the longer and more ridiculous the car, the more idiotic the pond life within it is likely to be. The Humvee limo was introduced for those who thought the traditional stretch limo was not quite macho enough, which is ironic as 'Humvee limo' translates as 'man with no penis' in several languages, including English.

LOCAL

Having a pub that you call your 'local' is still an important part of British life. The bar in question will be within a short walk or a brief drunken drive (going the back way and driving really slowly) of your home and should offer a refuge in times of marital disharmony, such as when your partner wants to watch *Desperate Housewives* and you want to watch the match. There should be the odd friendly face in there, even if it is only someone to nod at as you walk in the door. After all, this is not *Cheers*; everybody knowing your name

would just be intensely annoying. No one factor makes a good local, but the possibility of a lock-in (*see* LOCK-IN) should always be high on your list of priorities when assessing a new local if moving into a new neighbourhood. Recent immigrants can ask to be allocated a local at reception centres or via the Home Office.

LOCH NESS MONSTER

Scotland is home to one of the big three of possibly mythical super-monsters, with Nessie being right up there with Big Foot and the Abominable Snowman (or Yeti, as his PR team have re-branded him of late. Market research found 'Abominable' just a little too negative). Thought to be over 40 feet in length, the Loch Ness Monster has been part of British legend since at least the sixth century though with the development of photographic and moving film technology the sightings were given more credence in the carly twentieth century. Many of the main sightings have been proven to be hoaxes, but huge interest and research is still invested in the existence of the aquatic monster. It certainly brings in the tourists, with most gift shops in Scotland offering a range of Nessie tea towels, mugs and chocolates.

LOCK-IN

A long upheld riposte to Britain's (especially England and Wales') antiquated licensing laws, the lock-in is part ritual, part rebellion and part something to regret the next day. The lock-in is the illegal extension of pub opening hours, which

is signalled by the landlord rushing around closing heavy blackout curtains at around 11 pm. If you witness this it is your job to stay put and wait for any strangers to leave, whereupon the drinking will continue into the night. Some say the recent relaxation of licensing laws has spoiled the illicit thrill to be had from the lock-in or from visiting an illegal after-hours bar, so some landlords pretend to be serving you unlawfully even though they have applied for a late license. Landlords holding illegal lock-ins are always at risk from a visit from the police, but those least at risk are those who run pubs near police stations, providing late drinks to the local constabulary on a nod and a wink. If you are looking for an after-hours drink in a strange town simply head for the bar nearest the police station, knock thrice and use the well-established code words, ''ello, 'ello, 'ello' in order to gain entry.

LURGY

This frighteningly contagious disease is the kind of thing that spreads through British offices at an alarming rate, usually in the autumn or winter. Slightly worse than a cold, yet not quite as bad as influenza, symptoms of lurgy can include anything from a snotty nose and sore throat to an upset stomach or lethargy. The best treatment for lurgy is bed rest, which should be taken after phoning in sick and making sure you sound at your very worst. Lurgy is usually spread by sneezing or by that stinky woman from finance drinking out of your mug, though it can be passed from child to child by one touching the other and simply saying 'lurgy'.

M

MAGNA CARTA

This document from 1215 is perhaps given more importance than is relevant in modern times, as it was more a list of restrictions upon the power of the monarch than anything approaching a formal constitution (*see* CONSTITUTION). It certainly shaped the law and power within Britain, though, but not before King John, who was monarch at the time, renounced it and sparked off a civil war before the ink was even dry. Once this was resolved it was the perceived power of Magna Carta that helped to develop common law and the shape of legislation throughout England and then all of Britain. The right of Habeas Corpus is one piece of law that can be traced right back to Magna Carta and this is the understanding that no citizen can be held without trial or unlawfully imprisoned unless they look a bit Middle Eastern and the Americans say it is okay.

MARKS AND SPENCER

Not to be confused with *Communist Manifesto* writers Marx and Engels, this supermarket-cum-department

store is where Britain goes to buy its underwear. In fact, so widespread is this practice that HM Customs officials toyed with the idea of doing away with the checking of passports, simply checking the tag in the back of people's underpants instead. Those bearing some kind of M&S branding would be allowed in, while those wearing something more foreign or more racy would be denied entry. This would have had the dual effect of lowering immigration levels and maintaining the Right Kind of People in the UK, but the plans were shelved when it was revealed that the Queen has recently taken to shopping only at Primark and that the Prime Minister prefers to go commando.

MARMALADE

Our love of this citrus preserve is something of an anomaly in a country where it is not warm enough to grow citrus fruit, yet no traditional breakfast table would be complete without marmalade. We mostly favour marmalade made from Seville oranges, which has a slightly burnt and bitter taste, though lemon and lime marmalades are also acceptable, if you are a weirdo or an elderly lady. For connoisseurs, marmalade is all about the cut, which is a term for how chunky the preserve is and how much peel is included rather than how much glucose or scouring powder has been used to adulterate it. In this respect marmalade is quite different from Class A drugs, but its addictive and restorative qualities are similar. Note how Peruvian immigrant bear Paddington was always trying to get his hands on more

marmalade sandwiches and how much less maudlin he seemed to become once he got some. Most of his life was dedicated to getting his fix, though even he drew the line at those pathetic miniature plastic tubs you are given when you stay in chain hotels or rubbish B&Bs (*see* BED AND BREAKFAST).

MARMITE

Legendary for dividing opinion, so much so that its name can now be used to describe other things that polarise taste, this tarry-looking, brewing industry by-product is very much a savoury delight that you either love or hate. Made from the yeast that is used to turn sugar to alcohol in beer, Marmite is concentrated and has spices added before hitting the shelves. The wholly vegetarian (yet oddly meaty-tasting) spread can be smeared on toast, used in cooking or to make a nutritious hot drink. It should not, however, be used in the bedroom to spice up your love life. Marmite is also used as a key ingredient in one of the nation's best-loved snacks, Twiglets. These crunchy snacks are a favourite of curvy domestic goddess Nigella Lawson, who has been known to simply dip a catwalk model's arm in a jar of Marmite if she cannot find a packet of Twiglets when a craving arises. In 2006 Marmite introduced a squeezy plastic bottle, which was rumoured to be replacing the traditional glass jar that the brand is known for. The rumour proved to be fallacious, though this was not revealed before adults old enough to know better started bleating and blubbing about it on their blogs, like it was worse than 9/11 or having to meet Mick Hucknall.

MATHEMATICAL POSSIBILITY

This uniquely British aphorism neatly sums up the special kind of pessimistic optimism that surrounds potential success in sport, especially in football. Whether applied to domestic or international competition, the phrase is trotted out at that moment when nearly all is lost, yet some cruel possibility of success survives (*see* UNSWERVING OPTIMISM). There is a glimmer of hope that your team/country may win the league/qualify for a tournament, yet that glimmer depends on you winning your final game 12-0 and the worst team in the league beating the best, away from home and doing so by six goals or more. There could also be another side factor, such as another two teams drawing, your opponent being thrown out of the competition for use of nanotechnology or the discovery of time travel. Anything that could happen can be relied upon as a crutch in those hard, frustrating times. When it comes to even worse failure, there is the sister term 'mathematically safe', which describes the point in the football season when there is no longer a mathematical possibility that your team can be relegated from its league.

MILKMAN

The milkman, or 'dairy-based produce dispersal node' as they should probably be called nowadays, is very much an endangered species in our society, yet one we still hold dear to our hearts. This fondness is so strong that many of us feel inclined to beep and wave as we drive past the milkman

and his electric cart on our way to the out-of-town super-market where we buy our milk. Like the postman, the milkman provides a useful social service, for it is they who are often first to notice uncollected milk on the doorstep, which may mean an elderly customer may have fallen ill or passed away. These selfless vendors of semi-skimmed think nothing of breaking down a door and raising the alarm, having first rooted around the customer's stricken body to see if they have the £3.50 to settle last week's bill. The milkman is also a popular character in British comedy, often being seen as some kind of door-to-door lothario who has a regular appointment with any woman who has ever donned a negligee and pair of fluffy mules. Often jokingly said to be the father of unexpected babies or those who bear no resemblance to their father.

MINI

From its inception, this car showed off everything that was good about post-war ingenuity and invention in Britain, mixing style with practicality in a package that the whole world admired. Designed by Greek-Briton Sir Alex Issigonis, the Mini provided a practical, compact, fuel-efficient car and a fillip to the car manufacturing industry with its affordable good looks and ability to slip straight into the growing pop culture. Produced from 1959 to 2000, the Mini was seen as the antithesis of the American gas-guzzler and was associated with the swinging sixties, the best of British rally driving and landed high-profile roles in films such as *The*

Italian Job. The car's handling may not have been the best and it may have been a little cramped, but it has become an icon of Britain, as recognisable as Big Ben, the Routemaster bus or the Union Flag. After being killed off in 2000 the Mini came back in 2001 as a kind of evil, undead version. Now manufactured by BMW and much larger in size, the car looked similar but behaved differently, appealing almost exclusively to estate agents. What had once marked a Briton out as cool now marks them out as an arse.

MINI SKIRT

London designer Mary Quant is credited with kick-starting the sexual revolution with this minimal garment in 1965. Quant's chic innovation brought the skirt way up above the knees (which was something that men had been struggling to do on the back seats of cars since the 1950s) and left little to the imagination, with some christening the tiny garment the 'pussy pelmet'. The mini skirt was a boon to those who admired stick-thin girls with great legs that went on forever as well as for those who preferred homely girls with blotchy thighs. The mini skirt went on to become the official costume of Tyneside, where proud Geordie women can be seen celebrating their regional identity every Friday night in the pubs and bars around the Bigg Market. Local legend has it that if you hold back a mini-skirted girl's long hair while she vomits into the gutter then you will marry the following summer.

MODEL VILLAGES

These tiny replicas of the real world used to be a feature of almost every seaside town, capturing Britain in miniature and in time. Mostly built before the television age, the wooden models portrayed an idyllic Britain of village greens, bobbies on bicycles and people on their way to church in their Sunday best. The very best model villages had a model village of the model village in them, which in turn would feature the model of the model of the model village, and so on. In one case a model village model maker in Torquay was sucked into an infinity vortex and never seen again. Some model villages still survive, with the Bekonscot model village in Buckinghamshire being one of the finest examples. The village, which was built in 1929 features a tiny model of British literary icon Enid Blyton (*see* BLYTON, ENID) as well as some wonderful business names, like the firm of solicitors known as Argue and Twist.

MONARCHY

The debate over whether we should or should not have a monarchy in Britain looks no nearer to going away in the twenty-first century. As we are a constitutional monarchy (without an actual constitution) (*see* CONSTITUTION) the Queen has no real power, but she does get a good deal of taxpayers' money and as many stamps as she likes. Many say that the monarchy is outdated, outmoded and costly, though others claim that the monarchy is worth keeping for diplomacy, trade and tourism reasons. Personally, I believe

we should keep the royals but switch the funding from the taxpayer to the TV licence fee payer, with a one-hour fly on the wall-style update on BBC3 each night and a live online feed from all royal palaces and visits. Obviously Prince Philip would have to be kept locked up until after the watershed, but the entertainment, oddity and freakish behaviour would far outstrip anything that *Big Brother* or *The Osbournes* could muster. If things got dull then we could vote in new members of the monarchy, with Prince Doherty and Princess Winehouse being two obvious candidates.

MONTY PYTHON

Derived from the Latin for 'students will still be repeating this 40 years later and thinking they are hilarious', Monty Python was the name given to the grouping of six writers, performers and artists whose surreal sense of humour was allowed to run wild in the BBC television show *Monty Python's Flying Circus*, as well as in a number of feature films. Dispensing with the boundaries of traditional sketch comedy, the Python team created a safe interpretation of the satire boom, unwittingly creating memorable catchphrases and unforgettable sketches. Even now it is hard to talk about childhood hardship with someone intoning the Four Yorkshiremen sketch or to return a deceased tropical bird to a pet shop without suddenly realising you are banging it on the counter shouting 'wake up Polly' while you and the shopkeeper have fits of giggles. Many Americans believe that Monty Python is the only funny thing ever to have come out of Britain. This

explains why they always enquire 'What, like Monty Pie-Thon?' when you try to tell them about something both British and amusing, which is really fucking annoying.

MORRIS DANCING

Debate still rages over whether or not the name of the style of dance most associated with Britain (though it is more or less exclusively English) derives from 'Moorish dancing' or if it was simply dreamt up by some bloke called Morris who was a bit odd. But either way this complex mix of steps, stick banging and handkerchief waving has a pretty poor reputation among the natives. Visitors from abroad find it quaint and charming, as we do their national dances, but the combination of beards, flowers and bells is a turn-off for most Brits. Despite this general disdain, Morris dancing is on the rise again, with some goths figuring out that they may as well have a go, as they are already figures of fun. The sticks also come in handy for beating off teenagers who may attack them or ridicule their black, ragged outfits, with which they have replaced the traditional white Morris attire. A well-used anonymous witticism, often misattributed to Oscar Wilde, states that you should 'try anything once except incest or Morris dancing', which is easier said than done if you were born in Norfolk.

MUSHY PEAS

This gloopy accompaniment to fish and chips is made by soaking wholly unappealing sounding marrowfat peas

overnight before simmering them and adding a little sugar. Green food colouring is sometimes added, with mint being another possible addition for taste and colour, though this is horribly, horribly wrong. Some fancy restaurants will try to commune with the peasants by serving mashed petit pois as mushy peas, which should probably be a capital offence. For those who don't feel there are enough deep-fried components in their fish and chip supper, some takeaways offer the pea fritter, which is a wondrous fistful of mushy peas that have been battered and thrown in the fryer. Former Labour MP Peter Mandelson was said to have once confused mushy peas with guacamole, but this is an apocryphal tale credited to former Labour Party leader Neil Kinnock, who transposed the indiscretion of an American party worker to make it appear that Mandelson was out of touch with the common man.

MUSTN'T GRUMBLE

Oft-suggested as the two words that should be on a British coat of arms, this is a phrase that you will hear across the nation, especially when one Brit asks another how they are. The beauty of the phrase is that it is often used as the punctuation at the end of a lengthy list of complaints. 'Well, my hip's playing up again and you should have heard the noise from next door last night, mind you her at number 22 should do something about that gate, I think *Eastenders* is getting worse you know, my Jack has a cough again, have you seen the price of petrol? Still, mustn't grumble.' The phrase can also be a signifier of the stoicism that we are famed for

(*see* STIFF UPPER LIP), with many simply talking about their cancer or the wife they have lost before ending with a cheery 'mustn't grumble'. The use of the phrase was picked up by cockney music duo Chas and Dave, who recorded a song of the same name, which would probably make a passable national anthem.

NATIONAL ANTHEM

There is no denying that Britain's current national anthem, *God Save The Queen* – not to be confused with the Sex Pistols track of the same name, especially if you have them both on your iPod and have to play the correct one on an important public occasion – is a bit of a dirge. No one really knows who wrote it, so there is no one we can blame. Maybe if there were and we knew they were a nasty piece of work or, say, German then we might have an excuse to try out a new one. It has been around since at least 1744, though it is increasingly being seen to be the anthem of England and some parts of Northern Ireland, as Scotland and Wales have largely abandoned it for any national events. The Welsh prefer *Land of My Fathers* and the Scots usually plump for *Flower of Scotland*, and it is hard to blame them, especially as the sixth (largely unofficial) verse of *God Save The Queen* contains a line about crushing rebellious Scots. Alternatives such as *Jerusalem* and *Land of Hope and Glory* are often offered up as viable alternatives, though none seems to fit for Britain as a whole. Themes from *The*

Archers (*see* THE ARCHERS) or even *Match of the Day* could work and have the right upbeat feel, though it would be hard to trust anyone to come up with lyrics that would work for a twenty-first-century Britain. Monty Python's *Always Look on the Bright Side of Life* is another popular suggestion that crops up regularly, but not all Britons could manage the difficult whistling parts.

NATIONAL HEALTH SERVICE

The NHS was founded by the National Health Service Act of 1946 and was brought into being in 1948, with the aim of providing 'free' healthcare to anyone that needed it. The NHS is now one of the world's largest workforces, with around 1.3 million staff and a budget of over £100 billion, which is funded by taxation. Cuts in funding and increases in the services that have to be paid for are a constant political controversy, though our love of its nurses has been a constant throughout its existence and the largely female workforce are seen as both national treasures who deserve more than they earn and lightly-starched sex objects who might give you a quick flash as they empty a bedpan. This image was fostered by the *Carry On* series of films (*see* CARRY ON), which showed nurses in short, tight uniforms. Replicas in this style can now be purchased at the likes of Ann Summers, or so I am told. Those of a more 'specialist' persuasion will be reassured that these uniforms do come in Bernard Bresslaw size. Government ministers will sometimes use NHS facilities, rather than go private,

though only when they think it will improve their image and their ailment is no more serious than an ingrown toenail. These rare hospital stays also allow them to participate in experiments surrounding the efficacy of drinking nurse's urine in tea. Results are expected to be published anonymously on the internet somewhere around 2014.

NATIONAL LOTTERY

It has often been labelled a 'tax on stupidity', usually by those who have never experienced the thrill of getting four numbers quite near to the actual ones drawn out during a double rollover, but the National Lottery has become an integral part of our lives since the first draw in 1994. Many of us are members of a workplace syndicate, while others are casual players who only buy a ticket when there is a big win on offer. Obviously this is a completely illogical state of affairs, as these players are, in effect, saying that they can't really be bothered to win £2 million, but they might just manage to get out of bed and down to the corner shop if there is £5 million or more on offer. Since the launch of the National Lottery the game has expanded to take in several different drawers, with varying and increasingly complex ways of playing. This means that the draws themselves should take approximately one minute to complete, though the whole process is wrapped up in a light entertainment show that goes on for about six hours, or at least it seems that way.

NATIONAL TRUST

This society for preservation of monuments, buildings and countryside in Britain has become one of the largest landowners in the country since its inception in 1895. A National Trust sticker on a car is very much a middle-class signifier, which can move a battered Volvo or Morris Minor up the social scale. It says: 'Yes, my car may be falling apart, but I am your intellectual and moral superior'. During the Cold War a secret plan was hatched to only allow National Trust members access to nuclear shelters. This would guarantee a caring, middle class that would be able to rebuild the nation with dry stone walls and forge a better future through craft-weaving practices. Trust members were also considered the part of the population least likely to riot over food shortages.

NATION OF ANIMAL LOVERS

We are famed for being sentimental about soft fluffy animals as well as for the time and energy we devote to caring for our pets. In France, all animals are merely something to force-feed and then wash down with a glass of red wine; in Britain we buy them Christmas presents. Charities like the Royal Society for the Protection of Animals receive vast sums from wills each year and we have even started to feed cats and dogs with gourmet equivalents to our own ready-meals, and sometimes we even hide the packaging from them so they believe we cooked it ourselves.

NELSON

Admiral Lord Nelson, Horatio to his friends, is one of the most celebrated Britons largely due to his efforts in the 1805 Battle of Trafalgar, which lead to a victory over the Spanish and French fleets, as well as his own untimely demise. Nelson was seen as a master of battle tactics, with his head-on attacks confounding the opposition. His last words are often misquoted as being 'kiss me Hardy', but this was said sometime before he died from a bullet wound. His last actual recorded words were: 'Drink, drink. Fan, fan. Rub, rub'. Many British men repeat these words as a tribute to the great naval hero whenever they visit a lap-dancing club or massage parlour. The Admiral is immortalised in London's Trafalgar Square, where Nelson's Column features an 18-foot statue of him atop a 181-foot column.

NET CURTAINS

These flimsy pieces of fabric act as both social defence and helpful cover from which to spy on the neighbours. A decent pair (preferably from John Lewis) should prevent anyone from seeing in and realising what a mess your living room is in and also allow you to see exactly what it is that number 23 are having delivered. Nets of sufficient density should enable you to see boring neighbours or friends dropping by before they can see you, thus enabling you to perform the drop-and-roll manoeuvre, before crawling on your belly to the safety of the kitchen.

NEWSNIGHT

As well as actually being an intelligent news programme that covers world news and politics as comprehensively as it does home stories, *Newsnight* is a very British affair. Its principal presenter is the spiky Jeremy Paxman, who manages to combine being deadly serious with pugnacious fun as only a Brit can. Paxman often openly sniggers at the standard answers that come from politicians and in 1997 asked former Home Secretary Michael Howard exactly the same question twelve times in quick succession, with Howard squirming and trying to give a mildly different reply each time. The introduction of attractive economic editor Stephanie Flanders has even brought a flirtatious overtone to financial news, with many hoping that Flanders may eventually present a report from Paxman's knee. The highbrow show introduced a weather report in 2005, which was to replace the stock market report. This was treated with disdain by viewers and presenters alike, with Paxman once reporting 'It's a veritable smorgasbord. Sun, rain, thunder, hail, snow, cold, wind.' The weather report was dropped soon afterwards, proving that British maxim which decrees if you don't like a job then do it badly and in a really half-arsed way until someone else decides that it just isn't worth the hassle and asks you to stop.

NIGHTIES

The cold winter weather in Britain means that nightwear is often essential. For men, the choice is limited to pyjamas or a T-shirt and boxers, but women must make a choice that

will define them as either minx or matron. This is because the choice of nighties is limited to something revealing that will bring milkmen (*see* MILKMAN) to their knees or something in winceyette that can be used by the NHS as a visual antidote to a Viagra overdose. Doctors have found that adding teddy bears saying cutesy phrases to the garment can significantly decrease treatment times.

OAK TREES

The British love trees and every schoolboy is familiar with the dates when horse chestnut trees bear their fruit. But it is the oak that we hold in greatest esteem, admiring it for its size and power as much as its historical importance. It is most famous for being the kind of tree that King Charles II hid in when escaping from the Roundheads after the 1651 Battle of Worcester. The tree in question was then named the Royal Oak, inspiring a plethora of pub names. An oak was also said to have been the base of operations for Robin Hood and his band of outlaws and famous Brits have hiden in their branches throughout the ages; Edward Heath hollowed out a large oak near his home shortly after Britain joined the Common Market and David Beckham spent two weeks in one after his sending-off in the 1998 World Cup Finals.

OLD MONEY

Pre-decimal currency was a three-tier system of such inane complexity that even the simplest of purchases required a logarithm book, pen and paper to work out. German spies

during World War II were said to often hand themselves in when faced with the near-impossible task of splitting a bill into pounds, shillings and pence in the local tea rooms. This was especially difficult for the newcomer, as each coin had its own nickname, which often had nothing to do with its value. Working things out in old money is a favourite pastime of Britain's retired population, and they can often be heard exclaiming loudly how expensive something is when you recalculate it in old money. 'Thirty pence for an apple? You must be joking. That is two pounds, four groats and a cat's bicycle in old money. You could have bought this whole street for that back when I was a boy.' Pounds, shillings and pence were abbreviated to Lsd, which made even less sense than the bizarre system of how many pennies made a shilling and may simply have been a reference to the kind of drugs taken by the person who invented the system in the first place.

ORDNANCE SURVEY

We may only be a small island, but we do have one of the most thorough, accurate mapping systems in the world in the shape of the Ordnance Survey. As the name suggests, the maps were initially researched for military use, but they are now a trusted standard for walkers (*see* RAMBLING), surveyors and terrorist cells across Britain. This mapping began in the mid eighteenth century; the maps we know today started life in 1791 with the acquisition of an accurate theodolite. Theodolites have been used to survey ever since

and the twentieth century 'trig points' and pillars on high points that they could rest upon have become trusted landmarks for walkers, and inevitably, a growing number of spotters and enthusiasts count off these markers in notebooks as they find them. OS maps, as they are known, were used in the trenches of World War I, with special maps being commissioned to show the battlefields in which so many fell. Generations of children were taught OS map symbols in geography at school, which was fairly pointless, as the maps all come with a comprehensive guide to the abbreviations and symbols used. The only one most Britons remember from their schooldays is PH, which stands for public house.

ORWELL, GEORGE

Born Eric Arthur Blair (no relation to Tony), the unwitting creator of Jade Goody's celebrity and the gurning success of Davina McCall is best known for his novels *1984* and *Animal Farm*, the latter of which has given its name to both an animated film and a notorious bestiality video. But as well as being one of our greatest twentieth-century novelists, the Big Brother creator was a great writer and thinker on Britain, nationalism, patriotism and our way of life. Anyone doubting Orwell's Britishness (despite the fact that he was actually born in India) need only consider the fact that he took the time to write an essay on the correct way to make tea. He stood firmly against totalitarian regimes and even spied against those among his peers who were considered

political extremists. This collaboration with the state against alleged communists and his attendance at Eton make him a difficult hero for the left wing, though, equally, his socialist politics make him an unlikely hero for the moderate right. But both still regularly quote his works. The term 'Orwellian' has entered our language and refers to the kind of surveillance-heavy dystopia that many claim ID cards and blanket CCTV are leading Britain towards.

OVALTINE

We don't do excitement too well in Britain. You only have to look at Sir Alex Ferguson's awkward touchline celebrations when Manchester United score a goal to see that, as he tries to imitate what he thinks pure joy *should* look like. Catholic countries do it far better than we do, as we value reserve over enjoyment and a nice nap over festivals. Ovaltine is the national sedative that assures we stay that way. If we feel ourselves getting too emotional, thrilled or have simply drunk some real coffee then we can use the malted milk drink as a downer in order to bring us back to a dozy equilibrium. Rumour has it that the Government was considering introducing it to the water supply in urban areas in the early 1980s to quell the growing civil unrest. It is said to be the drug of choice for Radiohead. Horlicks is the alternative to Ovaltine and its name can also be used as a polite alternative to the word 'bollocks', which is ironic for a brand name that, as any schoolboy will tell you, sounds like oral sex with a prostitute.

OXBRIDGE

This conflation of the names of the universities of Oxford and Cambridge is a signifier of the interchangeability of our most famous educational institutions. Those who have attended either may be willing to attest to the greatness of one over the other, but for those who have not they simply represent the places where our political leaders and captains of industry come from. In recent years, moves have been made to make this pair of universities more inclusive of those who don't own most of the Home Counties and do not have some kind of distant chance of ascending to the throne should the Windsor's annual coach party beano to Bournemouth crash, killing all aboard. But the entrance exam for both does still include questions such as 'What part of India did your ancestors own?' and 'Who is your favourite polo player?'.

PAGE 3

First appearing in the *Sun* newspaper in 1969 and going topless the next year, Page 3 models hold a strange place in British culture. Appearing on page 3 from Monday to Friday, the young women showing off their breasts sit somewhere between saucy seaside postcard, sexy pin-up and girl next door. The practice has been heavily criticised by some feminists over the years, though some now see the models as the image of independent womanhood, as they make a very comfortable living from their modelling and other business interests. During the heyday of the Page 3 girl, Linda Lusardi and Samantha Fox became household names, appearing on chat shows and often being seen as clean-living role models. This trend toward acceptability has continued, with current favourite Keeley Hazell being lauded as an environmental role model by the Conservative Party leadership, as she insists that those photographing her use digital cameras rather than shoot with film and use chemical processing. Keeley has stopped short of advising readers to recycle their soiled tissues once they have enjoyed her latest photo shoot.

PANIC BUYING

We in Britain are blessed with a plentiful supply of most things we need and have a vast number of outlets that can provide us with anything from fresh fruit to a new computer, many of them 24 hours a day. But should we hear that any item, no matter how minor a part it plays in our lives, is in short supply then we rush out to the supermarket and join others in stripping the shelves bare. This in itself causes a shortage and so the problem goes on until someone in authority tells us that all is okay and that more Butterscotch-flavoured Angel Delight is in production as we speak, or that the story about bread being discontinued was just a rumour.

PANTOMIME

Deriving from the Italian word for 'out of work soap actor', pantomime has become a seasonal staple, keeping the theatres full and providing an income for that bloke who used to be in *The Bill* and that woman who you are sure was in *Emmerdale*, or was it *Casualty*? Panto season starts just before Christmas and goes on into the new year; the cast is made up of jobbing actors, reality TV floor scrapings and former stand-up comics who are camp enough to play the dame or rough enough to star as an ugly sister. Pantomime provides a kind of amnesty on failure, where the big fish who left town to fail miserably in the wider world is welcomed back with open arms as a local hero, even though he or she simply a former-weather girl from the

local news station. Pantomime gives you licence to shout in the theatre, with 'Behind you!' and 'Oh no he's not!' being favourites, though 'Oh Christ, this is still really disturbing, even after all these years' is most popular when panto regulars The Krankies appear on stage.

PASSPORT

As we do not have a written constitution, this document is really the most tangible totem of our Britishness, allowing us visa-free travel to all the places we have previously invaded and something to flick at the noses of petty bureaucrats the world over. Issued in the name of the Queen, our passport bears a message from her Secretary of State, requesting that we are given free passage and any protection or assistance that may be necessary, as well as the right to our choice of scented lubricants during a cavity search. The passport also bears a photograph of us looking really awful and, preferably, nothing like we actually look in the flesh. Controversy raged in 1988, when the UK passport was switched from the traditional blue hardback cover to a more flexible burgundy European model that is machine-readable. Many right-wing commentators saw this as the end of Britain, Empire and civilisation as we know it, but thankfully a middle ground was agreed. The solution was for those who get patriotically and overly upset by such things to buy leather or card pre-1988-style covers for their EU-model passports. These should be made in China and can be a fairly good guide of who to avoid sitting next to on a cheap flight.

PASTIES

Let's get this straight. A Cornish pasty should be made, sold and eaten in Cornwall. If you catch someone eating one on, say, a railway station platform anywhere else in the UK you should bat it from his hand, spit on it and then kick it onto the tracks. You will be doing them a favour. This traditional food of the Cornish tin miner combines meat, potato and onion in a pastry shell, with a crimp on the side that allows it to be eaten with grubby fingers before the crimp is thrown away as an offering to the mine's spirits. Pasties vary in size, with the traditional miner's version being big enough to serve as both breakfast and lunch. A number of variations on the traditional filling are acceptable, such as vegetable, cheese or even curry. A pasty should be eaten warm and should preferably come from a small baker's shop, not the fridge of a petrol station forecourt.

PEA SOUPERS

These thick, impenetrable fogs were a regular feature of urban life in the second half of the nineteenth century and the first half of the twentieth century, bringing with them respiratory infections, accidents and the perfect cover for maniacal serial killers. The pea soupers (dubbed thus by the *New York Times*) were at their worst in London, where overcrowding and the burning of fuel in homes and in power stations eventually lead to the Great Smog of December 1952 wherein Buckingham Palace was completely mislaid for two days and 40,000 fans turned out to see West Ham United

play a football match against what turned out to be two small boys and a dog. The match was abandoned at half-time when the referee realised that the opposing Fulham team had not turned up. The Clean Air act of 1956 did away with the smogs, moving power stations outside the cities and introducing smoke-free fuel zones. Some tourists are disappointed when they visit London and don't see the pea soupers they may have seen in films, though plans are afoot to rectify this in time for the 2012 Olympic Games: a giant dry-ice machine is set to participate in the rebranding of the Whitechapel area of London as The Fog Zone.

PEBBLY BEACHES

Being an island, Britain has a huge amount of beach, though a surprisingly large proportion of this is made up of pebbles rather than the fine golden sand we expect on a beach holiday abroad. We have learned to love the lumpy, uncomfortable surface they offer, with pebbly beaches like Brighton still being among our most popular. Pebble beaches often play their part in the class divide in Britain, with the fact that they are devoid of the donkeys (*see* DONKEYS), sandcastles and 'kiss-me-quick' culture that some find vulgar making for higher house prices and a more genteel atmosphere in the towns surrounding them. Others may suggest that the more middle-class settlements around pebble beaches simply reflects the fact that these home-owners feel safer in an atmosphere where no one can kick sand in their faces.

PERRY, FRED

The last British winner of the men's singles at Wimbledon managed an amazing hat-trick of wins in 1934, 1935 and 1936, twice beating Baron Gottfried Von Cramm and his evil Nazi henchmen. From this series of victories, Perry went on to become involved in sportswear by inventing the sweatband and then the distinctive cotton piqué shirt with the laurel logo with which his name is associated to this day. The shirt was taken up by fashion cults such as mods and skinheads in the 1960s and 1970s and the simple design is still the basis of a successful British fashion brand to this day. British tennis, however, has not been such a success and has not been similarly integrated into youth culture. Andrew Murray is the current British hope in tennis, though he may rapidly become known simply as a Scot by English fans if he does not win anything.

PIE, MASH AND LIQUOR

This traditional meal combination from London has been eaten since the eighteenth century and provides cheap nutrition for the working classes in the south and east of the capital. The pie is usually filled with minced beef and gravy, with both pie and mashed potato liberally doused in the parsley sauce known as liquor (some mistakenly think that the pie is served in a puddle of booze). Jellied eels are another popular accompaniment to the meal, providing a cheap source of protein in a disgustingly slimy package. London taxi drivers ensure that they eat this meal at least

once a day to keep up the mental and physical strength needed to simultaneously remember routes across the city and offer passengers insightful solutions to most of the world's problems.

PIERS

The seaside pier (*see* SEASIDE) has now outlived its use as a place for pleasure cruisers to land parties of daytrippers, but the iron and wood structures remain an important part of the architecture and atmosphere of our coastal resorts. Fifty-five piers still remain around our coastline, Southend being the longest, with most featuring a mixture of amusement arcades, fairground rides, food sellers, bars and theatres. Pier theatres are associated with comedy and traditional music hall acts, with the term 'end of the pier' becoming shorthand for a cheap, bawdy kind of show featuring saucy jokes, dancing girls and musical acts. These days the end of the pier theatre is likely to feature former Eurovision song contest entrants, stand-up comedians who have been axed from television and 1960s bands who have no original members left at all, though the bass player will be the original singer's second cousin's husband.

PIES

Pies are popular cheap fare in pubs and cafés around Britain, and each region have their own specialities, such as the flat, round pies of Scotland and the pork pies of Melton Mowbray. The popularity of pies in the UK lead to sand-

wich toaster manufacturer Breville introducing the Pie Magic in the 1990s, which was a home pie-making device. Sadly it didn't catch on, following pop-ska band Bad Manners' singer Buster Bloodvessel's idea for a hotel in Margate that served pie sandwiches 24-7 to the great pie idea graveyard. Pies are often eaten at football grounds, with the spicy chicken balti pie being one interesting recent development in what must be considered 'fusion cuisine'. The Fray Bentos tinned pie is the traditional Friday night meal for sad, single, lonely men who enjoy a dinner that looks a little like dog food with a puff-pastry topping.

PIGEONS

The way that you view pigeons is a signifier of where you stand in the class systems in Britain. If you race them as a hobby then you are working class, if you eat them in a jus then you are middle class and if you shoot them on your estate then you are upper class (the exception being if you are shooting them with a air rifle and your estate happens to be one that is owned by the council). Pigeon fancying is a big hobby among men in working class areas of Britain. The fancying bit is about them admiring the birds and preparing them for shows rather than them wanting to establish any kind of sexual relationship (usually).

PIMMS

Posited as the summer drink of choice for sophisticates, Pimms is, in reality, little more than a fancy alcopop (*see*

ALCOPOPS) for the middle classes. Mixed with ice, lemonade, mint, strawberries, oranges and lemons the drink seems like an innocent way to liven up a village fête or school fair, but the fact that it tastes like sweeties makes you forget how potent it is. This means that you then down glass after glass, leaving you to wonder if you really did make a pass at the vicar just before collapsing on to the tombola table.

POLICE
Famously unarmed, apart from when they are carrying weapons, the British police are known the world over for fairness, calmness and wearing a comedy replica of a breast on their heads. The service is run on a regional rather than a national basis, which can cause problems when major investigations inconveniently cross regional borders, though it also maintains a sense of being policed by your peers rather than an amorphous national body. Height restrictions for joining the police have been slowly phased out, meaning that constables of both sexes are now getting shorter as well as appearing younger. If current trends prevail then diminutive pre-pubescents will soon be arresting the likes of those of you who have chosen to shoplift your copy of this book.

POPPIES
Inspired by the dramatic red flowers that grew up through the disturbed earth in the fields of World War I, the Royal British

Legion adopted the poppy as its symbol of remembrance for those lost or injured in battle. Millions of paper replica poppies are sold each November; members of the public donate a few pence or a few pounds and attach the flower to their lapel in advance of Remembrance Sunday. Some see the red poppy as being a political statement of being pro-war, or possibly pro-whatever conflict Britain may be involved in at that time, but this feeling has subsided in recent years. Channel 4 newsreader Jon Snow recently caused controversy by not wearing a poppy. Most television newsreaders and presenters wear them in November, but Snow has spoken against the pressure to display any kind of symbol, no matter what its meaning. Recent health and safety initiatives mean that poppy sellers are no longer permitted to attach the poppy to buyers with a pin, though some World War II veteran sellers are ignoring this advice, especially when the buyer is an attractive young woman who needs assistance pinning the poppy to her cardigan.

POOR SERVICE

Despite glaring economic evidence to the contrary, we still see ourselves as a nation of industry and manufacturing, which means that we largely regard jobs in the service industry as being below us and not of any intrinsic value. This means that we are generally rude and discourteous to those who wait on our tables, serve us drinks or greet us as we enter buildings, with the result being that we then get poor service. But we generally see this as a good thing, even

rushing to go on nights out to restaurants that have legendarily bad service. Some restaurants in London's Chinatown are renowned for their disdain for customers, with many people travelling to them just be bossed around, insulted and served substandard meals. If you are going to irritate kitchen or waiting staff in Britain then you should always do this after you have eaten your meal, as you will end up eating at least 40% less faecal matter when dining out. Good service should be tipped, though bad service should be tipped more, for we are British and we don't like to be seen to make a fuss.

PORK SCRATCHINGS

These deep-fried pig carcass salted snacks are popular in pubs, where the greasy, hairy morsels can be washed down with beer in an attempt to stop them simply coming straight back up again. Known as the mildly more appetising 'pork rinds' in the US, the British name for the snack is thought to derive from the fact that they look a little like infected sores that a pig may have scratched off by rubbing itself against a wall. Health consciousness has made the fatty snacks less popular over the years, but they have outlived other similar products, such as Chicken Psoriasis, Lamb Lesions and Rabbit Herpes.

POT NOODLE

Invented for those who found Vesta meals too much like real food, the Pot Noodle requires only some boiling water

and a few minutes' wait in terms of preparation. Beloved of students and single men, the snacks come in a variety of flavours, all of which leave the consumer with a slight feeling of guilt and grubbiness. The branding gurus behind Pot Noodle took this feeling and ran with it, producing advertising campaigns that compared their food to a visit to a sex shop or a session with a kinky prostitute, only with more soya protein and monosodium glutamate. Pot Noodle, which was introduced to the UK in 1979, is now a staple of every corner shop (*see* CORNER SHOP), with some having special Pot Noodle filling stations for those who can't wait to get their dehydrated food home or those whose wives will not allow the plastic pots of noodley goodness in the house.

PRINCESS DIANA

The famously see-through skirted Queen of Hearts was a more regal, more legged version of Heather Mills-McCartney, who won over even the most ardent of republicans by being killed in a Parisian tunnel by hired assassins/our alien over-lords/accident (delete as appropriate) in 1997 at the age of 36. There was a huge public outpouring of grief over the Princess of Wales's death, with the event fundamentally changing the way that we mourn in Britain. Her untimely demise ushered in a more Catholic wailing and gnashing of teeth approach, where previously we had made do with a strong cup of tea and a short sit down. Many of us now remember her through the Sir Elton John song *Candle in the Wind*, which was a re-hash of

his song about Marilyn Monroe. The flamboyant singer got together with regular writing partner Bernie Taupin to bash out a quick adaptation, in much the same way that a lazy schoolboy may re-hash an old essay on the bus to school. The single stayed at number one in the UK for five weeks.

PROMS

This festival of classical music takes place for eight weeks each summer in London, building up to the Last Night of the Proms at the Albert Hall, which is the patriotic climax of the season. The Proms appeal to a wide variety of music lovers, though the Last Night audience is seemingly made up of braying inbreds who play out a bizarre series of rituals while dressed head-to-toe in items made from the Union Flag. The Last Night begins with *Land of Hope and Glory* and finishes with *Jerusalem*, which gives the evening the air of a Thatcher-era Conservative Party conference, only with less chance of it all ending with some harsh new laws on trade union activity or everyone laughing and pointing at Neil Kinnock.

PUB CRAWLS

So called because crawling is all you should be able to do by the end of the night, this fine tradition has long been a Friday night pursuit that is followed by manual labourers, students and hen parties alike. All you need is a few pubs within staggering distance of each other and you have your crawl. It is exercise and drinking combined. Imagine that.

Crawls can be arranged around themes, with A-Z and Monopoly board pub crawls (ie visiting a pub in each of the streets listed on the board) being popular in London, where the underground system can be used to hop around the city and to store excess vomit.

PUBLIC SCHOOL

Before public schools were legally recognised by the Public School Act of 1868, the children of the rich had to learn about sado-masochism, tuck and ruling the country on an ad hoc basis, picking up such knowledge where they could in the state-school system. This meant that they missed out on the chance to warm the toilet seat for older boys or for their buttocks to serve as an impromptu toast rack of a morning. Public schools are famous for their elitism, small class sizes and their ability to guide even the most dim-witted of aristocrats through A levels and on to their rightful place at an Oxbridge college (*see* OXBRIDGE). The existence of public schools is always a political hot potato; their abolition would have a damaging effect on the economy, with demand for trauma counselling and Soho dungeons all slated to drop by up to 75 per cent over a decade should this happen.

PUBS

The British pub should be a place of refuge from all the other worries of the world around you, be they those at home, at work or on a global scale. The beer should be good, the

service friendly and the crisps available in a variety of flavours. George Orwell (*see* ORWELL, GEORGE) probably came closest to the ideal of a British pub in his 1946 essay *The Moon Under Water*, which spoke of solid lunches and welcoming barmaids. Or was it the other way around? Whichever it was, this idea was taken and run with by the JD Wetherspoon chain who sell cut-price beer and who turned the idea into a kind of dystopian equivalent, where one-legged alcoholics squander their benefits cheques and are served by aspirant bar managers who are also on hand to dish out a bewildering variety of pre-prepared meals. The jam roly-poly of Orwell's dreams is nowhere to be seen. Still, there are some pubs that remain true to many of the *1984* writer's ideals. Mostly down backstreets and unsullied by the word 'gastro' as a prefix, these pubs serve up passable pies and a decent selection of beers, all accompanied by that wonderful traditional British pub sound: the absence of children.

PUB TRIPLES

Enter an establishment advertising cheap triple shots of generically named spirits and you know you are, almost literally, drinking in the last chance saloon. Gin, vodka and something that is certainly the same colour as whisky are all offered in huge measures for about the cost of a single slug of their household name equivalents, meaning that landlords can compete with supermarket prices and patrons can get hammered in a social setting. Spotting a sign offering such deals on the exterior of a pub is also a

good signifier that you may be able to find a friendly local drug dealer inside or even be able to buy back the contents of your garden shed if you speak to the right person.

PUDDINGS

The more refined may call the sweet course 'dessert', the less refined may call it 'afters', but either way, it is pudding that the true Brit should be after when the orders are taken. This catch-all term describes anything that could conceivably have been served after a school dinner and, mostly, anything that can be immeasurably improved by the addition of custard (*see* CUSTARD). So treacle sponges, jam roly-poly and chocolate sponge (with chocolate custard) are in, and gateaux, sorbets and cheesecake are out. Bread and butter pudding is the exception that proves the custard rule, while summer pudding proves that pudding need not be hot to bring pride to British hearts and stomachs. Friends who serve cheese and biscuits after a meal should be snubbed, or reported to the authorities. There is a direct correlation between time spent at public school and the desire for pudding, an equation that also works when measuring a fondness for spanking. Being spanked while eating a pudding is the ultimate fantasy for 62 per cent of Members of Parliament.

PUNCH AND JUDY

This puppet play celebrates the consumption of sausages, assault on police, wife battering and child cruelty and has subsequently been thrilling children nationwide since the

sixteenth century. The simple tale of a big-nosed, hunch-backed sociopath, Punch and Judy follows Mr Punch as he throws his baby from the window, sends his wife out after her and then batters anyone who gets in his way. This cast of victims includes a crocodile who steals his sausages, a policeman who comes to arrest him and the devil, who comes to take him to hell presumably to run some kind of training course in wrongdoing. The moral of the story seems to be that fecklessness and violence win the day, which has led some local councils to ban the shows from their beaches and parks. But in reality it is simply a grotesque cartoon-like slapstick, and children are unlikely to grow into crocodile-worrying murderers should they witness it.

PUNK

That the Union Flag and an image of the Queen were at the forefront of the music and fashion revolution that was punk shows you just how British it was, with bands like the Sex Pistols and the Clash still being cited as musical influences to this day. Retro rockers and Japanese fashion students don images of our flag and our monarch to summon up a punk look, with this image still doing so much for British tourism and business that the Department of Trade and Industry should probably add a safety pin to its logo. The music may have originated in the USA, but it was the marketing and design genius of Malcom McLaren and Vivienne Westwood that made it such a global influence, creating a year zero where rock dinosaurs and ageing Teddy

boys became seen as figures of ridicule and remnants of a distant past. With 50-year-old punks still donning the bondage trousers and with endless triple-album punk re-issues, live albums and best-of collections you could argue that nothing substantial has changed over the last thirty years and that punk has become assimilated by the status quo, though perhaps we shouldn't quite pronounce its spirit dead until we see Prince Harry sporting a pink mohawk and a Damned T-shirt.

QUEEN ELIZABETH I

Being the daughter of Henry VIII and Ann Boleyn, Elizabeth I was never going to be the poster child for well adjusted behaviour, though she did become known for her restraint in foreign affairs, adopting the motto 'I see but say nothing', which is similar to Arsenal manager Arsene Wenger's motto: 'I say that I see nothing'. Redheaded Elizabeth I could be fiery when provoked, though, and she is remembered most for being the monarch who oversaw the defeat of the Spanish Armada. She is also well regarded for allowing drama and literature to grow in Britain. Her fostering of the likes of Shakespeare and the dramatic fashions of her reign mean that her memory has been romanticised over the years and her period on the throne in the sixteenth century has been the subject of several films and costume dramas. Elizabeth I was sometimes known as the Virgin Queen due to her close friendship with Sir Richard Branson, the famed poet and explorer who introduced potatoes, tobacco and leaning trains to Britain.

QUEEN ELIZABETH II

The woman whose head is on our coins and stamps is seen as fairly moderate and tends to keep away from controversy in domestic and foreign affairs, though this is also due to the ever-decreasing role of the monarch in Britain (*see* MONARCHY), with it now being a largely ceremonial and tourism-attracting role. Apart from looking quite good on a tea towel, Elizabeth II is the current monarch of sixteen countries in the Commonwealth, top dog in the Church of England and, surprisingly, Duke of Normandy. This historical role now mostly pertains to the Channel Islands, though she is rumoured to sometimes dress as a man and impose new laws on this part of France when she gets bored with Prince Philip and the corgis. Our Queen famously had an annus horribilis in 1992, when most of her offspring were divorcing and separating from their spouses. Her annus was similarly nasty in 1997, when the public turned against her and her family for the lack of their public emotion about the death of Princess Diana. This was resolved when she returned from Balmoral and took a carriage to the local Texaco station to buy some carnations to leave at Kensington Palace.

QUEEN'S ENGLISH

Sometimes referred to as Received Pronunciation or even BBC English (*see* THE BBC), the correct enunciation of vowels and the ability to not drop aitches and then stick them on the front of words where they are not needed is

seen as vitally important in certain parts of society. In the upper class and parts of the middle class it is simply impossible for one to even consider dating anyone who has a glottal stop or who comes from Newcastle, as the voice is seen as a badge of breeding. The term can also be used with unintentional irony by rude morons who cannot understand what an immigrant or tourist is saying. 'We only speak der Queen's English, mate,' is one particular example you may hear in a bar or restaurant. In a further irony, the Queen herself only speaks German in private, though she is known to have a more than working grasp of Klingon, which she uses to communicate with Prince Charles when she doesn't want Prince Philip to know what she is saying.

QUEEN VICTORIA

The famously stone-faced Queen oversaw Britain's birth as an industrial nation and is often seen as the most fearsome monarch since the days of Henry VIII. She married her first cousin, Prince Albert of Saxe-Coburg and Gotha, following in a tradition that has kept European aristocracy in extra toes and webbed feet for the last 400 years. Never accept an invitation to enter a swimming race against the aristocracy, as they always win. Victoria was on the throne with the Empire at its peak and took Britain into the modern age, witnessing the start and growth of the railway and the first instance of the wrong kind of snow affecting the points at Clapham Junction. Her name is still attached to an era of advancement and achievement for Britain and it is for this reason that she is

probably the best-known British monarch globally. She is the only monarch to have a London Underground line named after her and she was apocryphally said to have not believed it possible for any woman to be lesbian, which has long been said to be the reason why this was not made illegal in Britain when male homosexuality was (*see* HOMOSEXUALITY).

QUEUING

If a person stands still for more than one minute in the UK then another will be drawn to line up behind them, with others soon joining them to make a queue. Honed by years of wartime rationing, the British queuing gene ensures that we are often at our happiest in a state of united anticipation. Where there are multiple queues we are able to make complex mathematical computations to work out which will move fastest and when a new product becomes available we will happily queue outside a shop for a special midnight opening, even though we could simply buy it in the morning. When faced with multiple options the true Brit should always form one queue for each outlet, so if there are three cash dispensers there should be three queues. The introduction of single queuing systems, such as in post offices and banks, threatens our way of queuing and our very way of life. It really is only a short leap from single queues and their hateful tethered posts to National Socialism.

RADIO 4

The word quintessential seems to have been made for BBC Radio 4's Britishness. It is hard to imagine the *Today* programme, *The Archers* or *Gardeners' Question Time* existing anywhere but on these shores and nowhere else in the world has a heavier concentration of plays about maidservants in peril. The station has a place for regional dialect, but it also retains a healthy number of presenters who speak only in Received Pronunciation and who still read the news in the traditional manner, from an ermine clad throne at Broadcasting House (*see* QUEEN'S ENGLISH). More British than the sound of leather on willow, this great British institution also rewards us with panel shows such as *Just a Minute* and *I'm Sorry I Haven't a Clue*. The latter is best known for the nonsensical game Mornington Crescent, though it is also loved for the laughter of genius comic Barry Cryer, whose guffaws often sound like a man in his death throes. Ironically, the show's consumer programme *Money Box Live* makes listeners long to hear their own death throes whereas *Quote Unquote* is actually blocked from

broadcast via the internet in Hungary, as it is deemed to be both depressing and disorienting.

RAIN

If you can see the Pennines it is going to rain, if you can't it is already raining. So goes the expression about the dampness of climate in the North West of England, though this constant expectation of rain exists in most of the UK. 'Looks like rain' is a constant refrain that can be heard as neighbours pass in the street or strangers converse in bus queues (those outside London, obviously. No one talks to strangers in London). Brits may moan about the rain, but we would not have it any other way and we fret if more than a week passes without a downpour. This concern extends to the summer months, when the ancient Pagan festival of Wimbledon (*see* WIMBLEDON) is held to mark the start of the summer and to pray for rain. Special rain dancers, called 'tennis professionals' are imported from around the world for this festival, to ensure rainfall and bring about a drought-free summer.

RAMBLING

A riot of kagouls, Thermos flasks, blankets and Ordnance Survey maps, this weekend pastime is one of Britain's favourite ways to pretend to be relaxed while actually making quite hard work of it. We don't do lying down and doing nothing very well (*see* DECKCHAIRS), as we don't want anyone to think we are Spanish or something. So our

enjoyment of our natural environment usually involves a ten-mile hike across a landscape filled with suspicious looking barrels of chemicals, rusting mantraps and fields containing agitated bulls. Despite its rather sedate reputation, rambling has a radical past, with the right to traverse rights of way and roam around our country being won by a long history of civil disobedience and campaigning.

READERS' WIVES

It may go against one of the Ten Commandments, but British men love nothing more than to covet another man's wife, especially on a Saturday morning when their own wife has gone out shopping. Ideally the wife in question should be inexpertly photographed on a patterned draylon sofa, in a room where the chintzy curtains are firmly drawn shut. It is preferable that flash photography be used, as this brings out a special shade of whiteness on areas of the wife that are rarely exposed to the sun. The selection of pornographic magazines that specialise in or include sections labelled Reader's Wives have recently proved to be quietly progressive in their outlook, meaning that a woman now need not actually be married to her partner for images of her bent over the ironing board to be included on their glossy pages. Similarly, there has been increased inclusion of a wider variety of interior design styles, so that men that hanker after seeing a slightly overweight Norfolk florist next to some half-constructed Ikea shelving are well catered for.

RED ARROWS

This crack team of stunt-flying RAF pilots have been a celebrated part of British life since 1965, appearing at special events and in fly-pasts, often trailing red, white and blue smoke. Their special skill lies in not crashing into each other while doing ridiculously difficult manoeuvres at high speeds, though, obviously, the subliminal thrill for those watching is the possibility that all nine of the distinctive Hawk aircraft might collide in a spectacular fireball somewhere over a car boot sale in Swansea. The pilots are all highly experienced and must have frontline experience, though the combat effectiveness of a group of highly visible aircraft trailing brightly coloured smoke has yet to be tested in a hostile situation. Leaked Ministry of Defence documents do suggest that deployment in a war may include the skywriting of disparaging messages and even the sky doodling of giant genitalia over enemy lines.

RHUBARB

The mildly poisonous pink rhubarb stems are to be found in many of our gardens and have also inspired one of our strangest fruit-growing practices: that of forcing rhubarb, which is associated mostly with Yorkshire. The fruit is grown in heated dark sheds, and the stems reach up for light above which makes for a more delicate flavour. Rhubarb and custard can be enjoyed as a dessert (*see* PUDDING) or as a classic boiled sweet, and these red and yellow jewels are just one of the royal family of British

confectionary, which includes sherbet lemons, kola cubes, wine gums and sherbet pips. The combination also gave its name to a classic BBC teatime cartoon, though Custard the Cat was actually rhubarb coloured, which twisted the minds of a generation and is possibly one major factor in the disintegration of society as we know it. Rhubarb crumble and custard is the dessert that 60 per cent of British men said they would like Nigella Lawson to cook for them if she was to invite them round for dinner. The other 40 per cent said that they would probably be too busy staring at her breasts to eat anything at all.

RICHARD, CLIFF

While America got Elvis Presley for their rock 'n' roll icon, Britain landed Cliff Richard. Attitude, sex and drugs versus being polite, going to church and remaining celibate. We did love and cherish Cliff for many years. We enjoyed *Living Doll*, *Bachelor Boy*, *Summer Holiday* (okay, okay, Melvyn Hayes' character was really irritating in that film) which became a perennial favourite and even *Devil Woman* wasn't bad. Though most of us did snigger quietly at *Wired for Sound*, Cliff's paean to the Walkman. But then came the Christmas singles, the singing at Wimbledon (*see* WIMBLEDON) and more bloody Christmas singles. The Peter Pan of pop became the pious pest and suddenly only 50-year-old women with an obsessive zeal for all things Cliff could bear his presence on radio, though that has not stopped him reaching the top ten.

RICH TEA BISCUITS

Previously advertised with the slogan 'A drink's too wet without one', these baked reminders of austerity enjoy a popularity that is far more about culture than taste. The adverts in question almost berated us for the sheer decadence of enjoying a simple cup of tea, as if the excess wetness may make us lose all sense of decorum. No, far better to abate the wetness with a cardboardy, sugary snack. Actually, take two. Spoil yourself. Just not too much. Don't you know there's a war on? At least there was until quite recently, you know. Rich Teas should always be dunked in tea, no matter what anyone says about manners. Just be careful to dip for just the right amount of time or you will be engaged in that very British pastime of fishing fast-disintegrating bits of biscuit from your cuppa with a teaspoon.

ROAST BEEF

Historians are not entirely sure when this became our national dish, but we have been known as consumers of beef since the Middle Ages, especially by the French, who often refer to Brits as *Les Rosbifs*. Usually served with Yorkshire pudding and roast potatoes, the Sunday tradition of a roast dinner is one way of ensuring that we consume enough saturated fat over the course of the week (*see* SUET). In times of war and poverty this will have been the one meal that Brits would endeavour to be able to serve meat at. Traditionally, the roast beef joint should be rested

for half an hour after it is taken out of the oven. This has no culinary benefit, it is simply how late most husbands are coming back from enjoying the Sunday lunchtime drink in the local pub or a round of golf.

ROBIN HOOD

Whether he was real, fictional or a folkloric amalgamation of several characters, the legend of Robin Hood has endured, having lasted since the early thirteenth century and has inspired many a television series. Thought to have been a nobleman who lost his land, Robin Hood was sworn enemy of both the Sheriff of Nottingham and 'King' John, though the persisting image of him is simply as a highly moral thief who took from the rich and gave to the poor. He is said to have hung around with his 'merry' men, though it is uncertain whether this meant they were a cheery bunch, a bit drunk or the UK's first all gay outlaw group. Hood is always cast as a sexy do-gooder in films and on television, though it is believed that his relationship with his supposed sidekick was not always as it is portrayed. Hood's close companion Little John is said to have been a *Ye Daily Mail* columnist who wanted to repatriate Friar Tuck to Eastern Europe and who regularly berated the liberal Hood for what he termed 'ye political correctness that hath gone mad'.

ROBINS

Though they stick around all year, these bright and cheery birds are the sweet-singing face of British wintertime, and

especially Christmas. Often seen on feeders and on bird tables, our red-breasted feathered friends delight us in the morning with their song, provide a nutritious between-meals snack for cats and are said to be accurate weather forecasters. They are the subject of the poem 'Who Killed Cock Robin' as well as the popular song 'When The Red Red Robin Comes Bob-Bob-Bobbing Along', which Charlton Athletic Football Club play before their matches. Two other teams, Bristol City and Swindon Town, are nicknamed The Robins. Killing a robin is said to bring very bad luck for anyone who does so, though, to be fair, it is probably even worse luck for the robin in question.

ROCK

No, not the music or the stuff that our homes sit on, but the confectionary that everyone brings back from the seaside (*see* SEASIDE). This is a uniquely British sweet treat, with the exact way that letters are put into the rock to spell out the name of the seaside resort you are in baffling even Stephen Hawking, despite his having repeatedly watched a documentary about it through the round window on *Playschool*. The brightly coloured sticks of rock come in a variety of flavours and colours and are almost entirely sugar, so you can feel tooth decay in action as you chew. Over the years, rude words and football team names have joined the names of towns as being popular things to spell out in sticks of rock. The same materials are also used to make dummies, imitation breakfasts and worryingly lifelike

genitalia for hen parties to suck on as they storm along the seafront at Blackpool. Though rock has always been seen as slightly crude, as exemplified by the George Formby song 'With My Little Stick of Blackpool Rock', which was clearly about something that rhymes with rock, but not at all about cheap sugary confectionary.

ROLLING HILLS

Like our weather, the landscape of Britain is interesting and varied. Sure, we don't have deserts, rainforests or seawater at a temperature that doesn't induce immediate male shrinkage of up to 60 per cent, but we do have some of the most beautiful countryside on earth. Chief among these areas of beauty are the soft rolling hills and undulating scenery that carries on the whole way up the country. These areas are prime locations for holidaying in Britain and also attract huge numbers of walkers, many attempting to tick off walks and collections of hills as noted by writer Alfred Wainwright. The fell-walking enthusiast has given his name to the peaks of the Lake District and popularised the Pennine Way by offering to buy a pint for anyone who finishes the arduous walk in its entirety. This is said to have cost Wainwright £15,000 and probably would have bankrupted him had he not died in 1991 before the onset of the £4 pint.

ROLLS ROYCE

This name may be as famous for aircraft engines as cars, but it is the luxury vehicles manufactured by Rolls Royce

that have become icons of Britishness. Never the most sleek, manoeuvrable or fuel-efficient, the Rolls Royce has long represented both aspiration and the brooding class war in Britain. It is the car that represents success and the car that is first to be torched in a riot situation. The crude, outsized nature of the cars makes them very visible signs of opulence, which is why they have traditionally appealed to working class celebrities for their bling factor. The famous silver lady that sits atop the distinctive radiator grill of each Rolls Royce is called the Spirit of Ecstasy, which is believed to be due to the fact that a stolen one of these hood ornaments will fetch exactly the amount needed to buy one ecstasy tablet.

ROUNDS

Drinking in rounds has long been a complex form of social bonding in the UK and is sometimes fingered as the root of our binge drinking culture (*see* BINGE DRINKING). Essentially a friendly way of making sure that everyone pays their way, round buying quickly turns into a race to keep up with whoever is the fastest drinker in the group. This is fine with a couple of friends, but go out in a group of eight and you know before the evening begins that you may be in trouble. It is deeply un-British to skip a round and the round buying cannot cease until everyone has taken his turn at paying. The information pack for new immigrants to the UK rightly reminds new arrivals that it is more socially acceptable to sleep with your neighbour's wife than to not get your round in.

ROYAL MAIL

Postal workers deliver mail on behalf of the monarch, with each stamp bearing a likeness of the ruler of the day and post boxes carrying their initials. This regal connection allows postal delivery staff some royal privileges, notably the right to ignore the words 'Do Not Bend' and to jump over walls and walk across lawns where it will shorten their route. The ancient ways of postal delivery staff have been passed down from generation to generation and they have even developed their own highly secretive language, which uses patterns of elastic bands seemingly dropped randomly on the pavement and on doorsteps.

ROYAUME UNI

Britain may suffer from a confusing surfeit of names (*see* GREAT BRITAIN), but there is only one foreign language label that we accept and that is for just one night per year. The Eurovision Song Contest is the excuse for this embracing of a French interpretation of United Kingdom, with its simply befuddling mixture of camp, camp and more camp, with some confusing traditional folk music thrown in to add to the unsettling topsy-turvy world it creates. The contest also represents just about as much European intermingling and co-operation as the average Brit is willing to accept. Eurovision has become a big party night in Britain, as we revel in our inability to recreate the glory of our big Eurovision wins. The two crowning glories were those by Bucks Fizz, who distracted the whole of Europe by

tearing the skirts off the female members of the group, and Brotherhood of Man with their distinctly 1970s song about kissing three-year-olds.

RUDE VEGETABLES

In most countries, seasonal vegetables are celebrated in any number of meals or side dishes, but we in Britain have found a far greater use for the produce of our soil and our toil. Instead of cooking our vegetables we find the ones that look most like genitalia and then laugh and point. This tradition started on BBC show *That's Life*, where Cyril Fletcher was employed as vegetable correspondent. His regular slot led to the successful spin-off show *Cripes! That Looks Like a Willy*, which was hosted by Fletcher and a young Angus Deayton. Fletcher left after the third series, when fruit that resembled breasts was introduced to the show. The traditional old comedian felt that this was beyond the pale and resigned. The show never aired again, but the tradition of rude vegetables lives on in the tabloid press, where a slow news week can be enlivened by a limp leek or deformed marrow.

RUGBY

Founded by an annoying idiot and in the spirit of cheating, the game of rugby has developed into two very different class-based strands since William Web Ellis first decided to pick up the ball and run with it during an early game of football at Rugby School in 1823. Can you imagine how irri-

tating that was? 'Oh, I am going to make my own rules up now, I am so great and I am doing my own thing.' At most schools this would have earned Web Ellis a slap at least, but as this was a posh school they decided to celebrate his unorthodox approach by adopting it as part of their rules. The games of Rugby Union and Rugby League are similar in style, but the former is more associated with the public and grammar school system, whereas the latter was traditionally the professional version of the game, which was more popular in northern working class towns. The exception to this is in Wales, where Rugby Union is played by all classes, though both codes now have a professional element. All the countries that make up the UK play rugby to a high standard, with followers of the sport being well known for their love of excessive drinking and dangling their genitalia into each other's beer.

ST ANDREW

Born on the Sea of Galilee, the Apostle St Andrew was about as Scottish as a nice healthy salad and a fresh glass of carrot juice, though somehow his death became celebrated in both the Scottish flag and the Union Flag (*see* UNION FLAG). St Andrew is not even rumoured to have visited Scotland, though some relics of his unorthodox crucifixion cross are believed to have made it to the country around the tenth century. This X-shaped design became the basis for the St Andrew's cross, which is what we see on the blue-and-white Scottish flag today and which makes up a part of the Union Flag. The fisherman, who is celebrated in Scotland each 30 November, didn't want to be crucified on the same shape of cross as his friend Jesus, no, he wanted to be different, so the distinctive shape was used for his execution. It is a good job that not everyone was as fussy, or the whole crucifixion industry would have been in chaos. After all, there are only so many shapes you can make from two pieces of wood and a handful of nails.

ST DAVID

The Welsh are rightly proud to have a patron saint who is a native son, with St David having been born in Pembrokeshire around the year 500. What is not so clear is what they think of him being a beer-denying, vegetarian hippie who preached that possessions were wrong and that men should pull ploughs rather than animals. St David was a teacher and preacher, who lived a frugal life alongside his monks; his most celebrated miracle was his supposed raising of a hill below his feet at Llanddewi Brefi, so that the audience could see him preaching more clearly. St David's Day is celebrated on 1 March each year, which is said to be the day of his death. Welsh people wear either a daffodil (*see* DAFFODILS) or a leek to mark the day, with the latter perhaps being a reminder that they are at least able to eat things other than just leeks now that he is not around to tell them off.

ST GEORGE

Possibly a Turkish Christian who slew a dragon in Libya, possibly made-up and possibly any number of things; one thing we can be sure of is that St George was not British, English or connected to the UK in any tangible manner. But, that said, St George has come to represent the spirit of the English, be it in battle, in sport or in slaying dragons. These days those dragons are more likely to be metaphorical than actual, largely because dragons are not actually real. St George's Day celebrations have enjoyed a small resurgence

of late, though until it becomes a national holiday it is unlikely to match the scale of festivities around St Patrick's Day in Ireland, or even in parts of north London. The English are only too happy to spend the day in the pub, but not en masse at the expense of a day's annual leave on 23 April.

ST GEORGE'S FLAG

This once almost forgotten flag has recently come to symbolise far more than a dedication to all things English or the celebration of England's patron saint. The red and white flag swept England in 1996 as the Euro 96 football tournament gave a new popularity to the sport, which had hit rock bottom just a decade earlier due to hooliganism and poor performances by the England team. In 1966 England's players ran out onto the pitch to fans waving Union Flags, but in 1996 there was a sea of red-and-white. By 2002's World Cup, the idea of flying the flag had really taken off, with plastic versions adorning every white van in the country. By 2006 the Prime Minister was flying the flag over Number 10 when England's World Cup matches were being played, denoting that he was down with the common man and was not to be disturbed while watching the game on TV, unless it was by someone bringing more lager or crisps. Since 1996, the flag has become seen to be something that denotes the tastes of the lower orders. While The *Sun* gave away flags and posters featuring the flag, The *Guardian* carried articles debating whether flying the flag from your car was a bit too chav and what the environmental impact might be.

ST PATRICK

Known to most of the English-speaking world as the patron saint of Irish stout and green lager, St Patrick is the saint for the whole of Ireland, including the North/Ulster, though it is unlikely that you will see Reverend Ian Paisley wearing a giant Guinness hat and singing 'Danny Boy' on St Patrick's Day, which falls on 17 March. Born in the fourth century, St Patrick is best known for banishing the snakes from Ireland, which was actually a fantastic scam, as Ireland didn't really have any snakes at the time. I myself banished rampaging lions from Dorset, but did anyone appreciate my efforts? Well, no. St Patrick's Day is thought to celebrate the date of St Patrick's death. He was born in Scotland, probably to a Roman family, before being taken to Ireland as a slave where he then became a preacher.

SAYING HELLO

In British society there are very strict rules on conduct and, especially, on how and when you should greet your fellow Britons. These rules state that you should not say hello to anyone on the London Underground, even if you know them, though you are permitted to greet all and sundry if you are a Yorkshireman on his annual trip to the big city and are out to prove just how 'bloody unfriendly' everyone is. Conversely, you should always say hello to everyone if you are in the countryside. The countryside includes that little bit of scrubland behind the council flats where you walk the dog. On busy weekends in beauty spots this means that you

will spend more time greeting fellow walkers than enjoying the view, but you will continue to do so anyway, lest anyone think you rude or foreign.

SCHADENFREUDE

It is said that we use this German word because there is no direct, pithy equivalent in the English language that means 'taking joy in the misfortune of others'. Obviously we could have thought of such a word by now, but this usage remains to remind us that it is the misfortune of the Germans that we enjoy the most. From economic downturn to car manufacturing errors and footballing setbacks, nothing brightens a Brit's day like turning on the morning news to be greeted with a story about Germans in distress.

SCONES

These small buns may be the centrepiece of any cream tea, but they are also the item that conjures up most lingual debate within the UK. Arguments rage as to whether you should say scone to rhyme with 'gone' or to rhyme with 'bone'. Those who say it one way will claim that anyone who uses the other is either posh or common, depending on how they identify themselves (*see* CLASS). 'Scone' defies regional accents, unlike obvious north-south divide words such as 'bath' and 'affordable housing'. Scones can come plain or with added fruit and should only be eaten with clotted cream, which is named after the state it leaves your arteries in.

SEASIDE

Being an island nation, we are never more than a short drive from the seaside, which is naturally one of the first places that our leisure industry evolved. We rapidly went from bathing machines to kiss-me-quick hats and saucy post-cards, identifying the water's edge as a place where inhibitions could be cast aside. It may have lost some of its allure in the twenty-first century, but it is still the place we go to make sandcastles, ride donkeys and catch crabs, be it in a bucket, from the bed in a B&B or from a local heroin-addict prostitute.

SHAKESPEARE, WILLIAM

The Bard, as he is popularly known, was born in Stratford-Upon-Avon in 1564, though not on 23 April as is commonly held to be true. This fallacy was simply a neat way of tying his birth to St George's Day, which was the date that he died in 1616. No one knows the date that William Shakespeare was born, with doubt even being cast upon whether the man born in Stratford was the man who wrote all those wonderful plays and sonnets. Nevertheless, the work of Shakespeare continues to be regarded as beyond reproach and is taught in schools, often to the exclusion of more modern literature that has less snob value attached to it. *The Complete Works of Shakespeare* is always given to those who the BBC make virtual castaways on the radio programme *Desert Island Discs*, though most would probably prefer *The Sopranos* box set and a DVD player really. Philistines.

SHIPPING FORECAST

This round up of wind speed and weather conditions in our coastal waters is read nightly on Radio 4, informing the middle classes that all is well, even if sailors are enduring a force nine gale in Cromity. Because the forecast is read as a kind of poetry, the words just wash over the non-marine listener, allowing them to ignore the actual weather predictions and just imagine some rustic-looking boats bobbing around in a gentle swell. They are happy to believe that those jolly sailors are probably wearing a striped Breton jumper, perhaps smoking a pipe. In fact, what the average listener half hears as they down their cocoa could probably be summed up as: 'World not blown up yet. Good'.

SHOCK JOCKS

Although the idea of the combative radio presenter is an import from the US, circumstance has made this medium our own, with presenters like Jon Gaunt and James Whale providing a more down-to-earth alternative to the measured debate of Radio 4. Essentially a modern form of jousting, shock jocks witter on about anything they know will get their listeners riled enough to call in, with the result being that the callers usually engage in battle to see who can shout loudest. The rules of engagement mean that the debate is effectively over as soon as anyone uses the words 'Nazi' or 'politically correct'. The winner in either case is, of course, the shock jock, as well as the radio station, which is making cash on each call. The rise of the shock jock

coincided with the introduction of the Mental Health Act 1983, which meant that unstable insomniacs were removed from hospitals and reintegrated into society, providing a steady stream of punters who could scream down the telephone about black helicopters and immigration until the breakfast news teams arrived.

SKIN

We may see ourselves as a vast mix of different races and skin tones in Britain, but the 2001 census showed that 92 per cent of the population is white. This means that we are mostly a pasty collection of potential skin-cancer patients who look ruddy and red-faced in winter and sunburnt red in the summer. Hundreds of years of being invaded by the most pigment-free of races in Europe has ensured that at least 3 per cent of Britons are now born entirely transparent. We really should have spent more time in bed with the Romans, as at least this would have cut down on the cost of endlessly buying Factor 60 sunscreen the moment that the slightest hint of sun appears. Many Brits are seeking a solution to their freckly, lard-like skin in the instant tanning salons that are springing up in our town centres. Visitors can ask to be Dale Winton Orange, Jordan Tangerine or, bring in some fried chicken or a Scotch egg and ask the assistant to try to match the colour. Britons of Celtic heritage are at most risk of sunburn in the summer months and there are plans to put a retractable roof on Belfast, which can be employed like a giant parasol during July and August.

SMASH

Somewhere on Mars a television advert is screening, which portrays idiot Martians neglecting the health benefits of proper cooking with fresh vegetables and instead making instant mashed potatoes with boiling water while humans look on and laugh. Or at least that is what I like to think. The Smash Martians advert, where the Martians laugh at the humans for making real food and not super-advanced instant mash potato space food, is one of the best-loved British television adverts of all time and heralded the arrival of fast food in the home. Smash also makes a decent wallpaper paste if you get the consistency right, though it should not be used for grouting.

SOCKS WITH SANDALS

This wonderful confusion about continental footwear has been perfectly captured by photographer Martin Parr, portraying the British male's unease about public nudity, even if it is just the toes. Usually seen on middle class, middle-aged men in the height of summer, the socks and sandals combination is a look that says: 'Yes, it is very warm, but I am not a savage'. The natural habitat of this kind of gent is in the car park of a beach or beauty spot, looking in the opposite direction from the main attraction. As this look becomes increasingly rare (largely due to the free-love laxness of the Birkenstock), spotting it in the street is becoming a nostalgic delight, like spying a Morris Traveller or a child with rickets.

SOUNDS OF BRITAIN

We are not a nation that likes to get het up and run around shouting too much, so the sounds that sum up our isle are those that come between moments of pure peace, or those that don't interfere with it too much. So, the sound of a lawnmower being pushed across grass, the thwack of leather on willow (*see* CRICKET) and the snatch of evensong as a late arrival opens the church door are all sounds that swell our hearts. The dawn chorus is another sound that can stop us for a moment and make us consider our place in the world as can the distant sound of an ice-cream van or even the singing of 'Abide With Me' at an FA Cup Final. Obviously not all British sounds are desirable ones, for example, the approaching boom of a car almost entirely constructed of bass speakers, the clang of the bell for last orders at the bar or the sound of our neighbours having noisy, energetic sex as we lie in bed with a snoring partner.

SOVEREIGN RINGS

Though the wearer may believe that their wearing of the sovereign or half-sovereign ring marks them out as a man or woman of means and sophistication, the rest of us simply assume that they are displaying some kind of pride in catalogue shopping. Ubiquitous among the underclass (*see* CHAV), the sovereign ring does mark out status in this group. The ring informs fellow members that this person currently has the financial wherewithal to not to have to pawn it at Cash Converters and is also probably quite handy

in a fight. Multiple rings can also be seen as battle medals, denoting that the owner has possibly had the fortitude to queue in Argos on more than one occasion.

SPARROWS

We are not alone in being able to spy these cheery brown birds in our gardens, but our love for the sparrow has seen us christen it the 'Cockney sparrow' as well as follow with concern its lessening numbers in our cities. No one quite knows the full story of how the birds came to be known as Cockney sparrows, but it may have something to do with them being short, cocky fellows who like a singsong, stick their chest out and are fond of a dust-up. In recent years the sparrows have been following the old cockneys from the east end of London and are now more likely to be found in Essex, where they nest in imitation designer handbags and have adapted to survive on a foraged diet of discarded hair extensions and a kind of lichen only found on gatepost lions.

SPITFIRE

Star of the Battle of Britain (*see* WORLD WAR II) and recurring symbol of British defiance, the Supermarine Spitfire is a single-seater fighter plane whose elliptical wing design has been imitated by the outstretched arms of small boys throughout the nation since it first appeared in the skies in 1936. Designed by R J Mitchell, the Spitfire was the scourge of Nazi Germany's Messerschmitt 109 and a true icon of

hope in World War II. Sadly, our skies are now defended by far less romantically named aircraft, such as the Eurofighter, which is made entirely from recycled staples that were once used to bind EU treaties together.

SPOTTERS

Whether you look at the end of railway station platforms, the perimeter of airfields or the outer reaches of bus stations you will find that most British of hobbyists, the spotter. Armed with notebook and pencil, these teams of numerical obsessives spend most of their spare time in the pursuit of numbers, be it noting down the figures on the side of a diesel engine or trying to catch them on the underside of an F-15. Spotting does go on in other countries, though not to the extent that it does on our shores, and it fulfills our quiet need for order. In Greece, the idea that grown men would travel across Europe to write down aircraft numbers seemed so alien that a judge incarcerated one group of British spotters as spies. Spotter spotting is becoming an increasingly popular hobby among train spotters or bus spotters who have spotted all there is to spot.

STAG NIGHTS

While America has the more sedate-sounding bachelor party, we give a more accurate name to the festivities that the groom enjoys in the run-up to his wedding. Traditionally held on the condemned man's last night of freedom, stag nights have now moved to the weekend before the actual

wedding, which reduces the likelihood that the groom will throw up on the bridesmaids or have to call in his excuses from a police cell. The 'stag' name refers to the rutting, fighting and stumbling around that the night entails. It is not clear whether actual stags can drink 12 pints of strong lager, all of which have been spiked with vodka by their mates, though that may actually make an interesting experiment, or even a half-decent reality TV show. A 'good' stag night will involve the SAS being called out to deal with your out-of-control party, and the groom winding up tied naked to the masthead of a trawler heading for Norway is also acceptable. Death of the groom is frowned upon, though a broken nose or STD is a badge of honour for the stag.

STIFF UPPER LIP

One of the great British characteristics, the stiff upper lip refers to the un-trembling reaction to any number of misfortunes or disasters that may befall us, individually or collectively. 'Yes, my house burnt down last night, but of course I will be going into work today. Obviously my wife would have gone in to work too, had she not perished in the blaze.' During times of war or economic strife, the stiff upper lip has held us together as a nation where other lip-flapping nationalities would panic and run around screaming. Some may say that ulcers, irritable bowel syndrome and post-traumatic stress disorder are all side effects of this unflinching outlook, but they should really stop being so emotive.

STONEHENGE

This crumbling ancient monument is one of the must-see sites for any tourist visiting Britain from overseas, as it is the most celebrated of our island's many stone circles. Much speculation is made by historians and religious groups as to how and why it was built, but the fact remains that this national treasure is broken and badly needs replacing, perhaps in a location that is more easily accessible or has a need for extra tourists. As it is, the tumbledown circle is not fully open to the public apart from during the summer solstice, when it crawls with hippies, crusty punks and soap-dodging Special Brew drinkers who imbue it with a spiritual significance not too dissimilar from that of its other big fans, the Druids. A new Stonehenge, complete with intact lintels and no toppled stones, could be used to enliven the economy in one of our fading seaside towns; Weston-Super-Mare is one likely candidate for monolithic regeneration.

STRIPPERS

Before pole dancing and lap dancing clubs became upmarket venues to which it is acceptable to take business contacts or to tell friends you spent your Friday night at, there was the strip pub. This was a uniquely British venue where you could have a pint, some pork scratchings and watch an eczema-suffering mother of three remove her clothes in a manner that managed to be both perfunctory and mildly threatening. Entry to most of these venues was

free, though you were encouraged to drop a 20p coin into a pint glass as the stripper went around the room before she started the performance. Presumably this was because you probably wouldn't be willing to pay afterwards, as you would then know her torso was covered by a bad prison tattoo of an eagle fighting Bart Simpson above the crossed-out name of a former boyfriend. On the up side, some of these venues do offer free roast potatoes on Sundays.

SUET

This dried beef or mutton fat is an essential staple of British cooking and has been furring up the arteries of the nation since time immemorial. It is used with a mixture of dried fruit in Christmas pudding and forms the basis for other hefty desserts, such as spotted dick and treacle pudding, but it is in its various savoury applications that the saturated fat is at its most resplendent. Mixed with flour and steamed, it forms the outer casing of steak and kidney pudding and, most importantly, it is also an ingredient in dumplings. No stew from any corner of the British Isles is complete without these fluffy, doughy balls to soak up the gravy and its flavours. A suet-based main course should always be followed by a suet-based desert, which should be followed by a long lie down and/or a trip to the cardiac unit at the local hospital. Lower fat vegetarian suet is available for those who wish to draw out the process of dying slowly from coronary heart disease, though some claim that the

extra years of life do not compensate for the lack of a beefy jam roly-poly on a winter's evening.

SUNDAYS

As Britain is still officially a Christian island, Sunday is our official day of rest, though more recently it has become a day of stress. Sure, most of us don't have to get up and go to church any more (unless we are planning to get married in one soon), but we have somehow conspired to make it more stressful than a normal working day. Leaving the house at 7 am to be able to get on the golf course/join the queue at Ikea/fetch building supplies for that new bathroom that will 'add value', you bump into the paperboy, who is trying to cram six pounds of newspaper into your letterbox. The mangled pile of paper contains one 'broadsheet', one mid-market paper and one tabloid. Upon your return you have to plough through thousands of words about world economic meltdown, the falling value of your house (and why that may be linked to the death of Princess Diana) and how your football team is about to sell their star striker. And this is all before you have started the four-hour preparation of Sunday lunch or picked up the in-laws from the station. Monday morning seems sweet relief by comparison.

SWINGING SIXTIES

'If you can remember them, you weren't there,' goes the phrase most associated with the period that saw sharp suits, free love, the Mini, the Pill and Twiggy all come to the

fore in London's Carnaby Street. Naturally, the phrase also relates to the large amount of marijuana and psychedelic drugs that were doing the rounds at the time and it was a largely fallacious soundbite. Actually, the saying has more truth today: many of those who were at the centre of the fab, groovy happenings now have trouble remembering where they put their keys and whether or not they left the grill on, never mind whether it was Dave, Dee, Dozy, Beaky, Mick or Tich they shared a bed/a pint with. Yes, the generation that hoped it died before it got old has started to look at catalogues for incontinence pants.

T

TABLOIDS

The small format newspaper, also known as the red-top has long been an institution, providing a breakfast table combination of news, gossip, sport and candid pictures of members of Girls Aloud. The most famous of these are the *Sun* and the *Mirror*, which have traditionally been seen to hold diametrically opposed political views. However, the *Sun*'s backing of Tony Blair in 1997 saw a sea change in the notion that the *Sun* was Conservative and the *Mirror* was Labour in leaning. The papers are famous for uncovering political and personal scandals, as well as for amusing and alliterative headlines, some of which use double entendre. Many 'quality' newspapers use the tabloid format in some way now, though they tend to give the size fancy names so that readers don't buy them expecting news on the wrong kind of Jordan.

TEA

Nothing is more British than a cup of tea. Not even Stephen Fry wrapped in a Union Flag, riding Reverend Ian Paisley over Ben Nevis while eating roast beef with All The

Trimmings and flagellating the shouty Ulsterman with a leek. Originally discovered by chimps wearing human clothes, tea is said to date back 4,000 years, but it wasn't until it was imported into Britain in 1660 (when King Charles II first uttered the words 'Stick the kettle on, love') that anyone started to drink it properly. Enjoyed with as few as four biscuits, tea is the item that most Brits take on holiday with them, usually in bag form. Americans, especially Madonna, are renowned for their inability to make a decent cup of tea, usually making it as weak as their currency and as lukewarm as their enthusiasm for Robbie Williams. Singer Boy George spoke for a nation when he said he would prefer a cuppa to sex. The milk in first or last debate still rages amongst Britons. It is thought that more would turn out for a referendum to finally decide it once and for all than will turn out for the next general election.

TEA (AS A MEAL)
As well as describing our favourite drink, tea also gives its name to a confusing variety of meal breaks, times of day and ceremonies. It can mean an afternoon gorging on scones and cream (supplemented by a side order of cakes and small sandwiches), an occasion on the lawn with cucumber sand-wiches or a break in a cricket match. If you are working class you may call your evening meal 'tea'. If you are middle class you will call this meal 'dinner' and if upper class you will probably call it 'supper' and have your servants chew at least some of it for you first.

TEETH

Across the globe, and especially in the USA, the term 'British teeth' is derogatory slang, used to highlight an individual's rotting molars and gap-riddled grin. American schools are full of children wearing heavy braces on their teeth, but in the UK our children find that these get in the way of smoking and snogging. National Health dentistry had started to rid us of this image somewhat, though the difficulty of finding an NHS dentist now means that our teeth are getting worse, with some turning to pulling out their own rotting incisors. Rumour has it that the abandonment of NHS dentistry is actually part of a wider government plan on tackling obesity, the argument being that if all you can eat is soup or smoothies then you will eventually lose weight.

TELEPHONE BOXES

The famous red telephone call box, designed by Sir Giles Gilbert Scott, is a proud totem of Britishness that tourists flock to be photographed in or standing next to. The red K2 boxes were introduced in London in 1926; red K6 boxes eventually hit streets in the rest of the UK from 1935. Obviously, no self-respecting Brit would be seen dead in one nowadays as we all have our own mobile phones. Their primary use is as urinals, but some foreign visitors do use them to make calls, mostly to the prostitutes who advertise their wares in them on lurid calling cards. In 2004 it was discovered that most of London's top crack dealers use the

boxes for their trade. Trading floor gossip stating that British Telecom were to get a cut of these deals caused shares to rocket in late 2006, but the whispers turned out to be untrue. BT chiefs are rumoured to be considering a filtration system that can extract the nitrogen from the copious amounts of urine deposited in telephone boxes each year. This could then be sold on as organic fertiliser. This process of 'extracting from urine' should not be confused with 'extracting the urine', which is a technical process BT initiates when customers request to move their broadband connection to a new home.

TENNENT'S SUPER

Starting out as a small Scottish brand that really knew its market, Tennent's initially issued regular strength lager in cans adorned with pictures of women who became more attractive the more you drank. This moment of marketing genius was surpassed by the introduction of the 9 per cent Tennent's Super lager, which is now favoured by an estimated 72 per cent of all tramps, street drinkers and itinerant dipsos in the UK. Tennent's Super established itself as the premier cru of tramp fuels in the face of fierce competition from Carlsberg Special Brew, although an early viral advertising campaign in 1987 was largely unsuccessful. Tennent's staff sent 12 of Glasgow's top tramps on the 6.15 a.m. train from Glasgow with instructions to spread the word to London's down-and-outs. Sadly no one could understand a word they said by the time they disembarked at King's Cross Station.

TEXTING

We were not the first nation to get excited about mobile telephones, but we were certainly the first to make texting take off in a big way. While the US and Japan are still all fingers and thumbs we have got to the stage where school children have abndnd mst vwls and society has advanced to deciding important things like the outcome of reality television shows by sending text messages. Obviously General Elections will come next, with instructions expected to include: 'To vote Conservative text 1; to vote Labour text 2; for Liberal text 3, to spoil your ballot paper with a scrawl about how the whole thing is controlled by the Freemasons and that the queen is actually a giant lizard text 4.' Government technical experts assure us this system could be safe and secure, though there is always the risk that crossed lines could see us install President Jade Goody somewhere around 2016.

THATCHER, MARGARET

The Grantham grocer's daughter first came to prominence in the 1970s, when, as part of the Conservative Heath government, she was responsible for ending free milk for schoolchildren. Left-leaning parents childishly nicknamed her 'Thatcher, milk snatcher', while children rejoiced that they would no longer be forced to drink lukewarm milk each day. She rose to Conservative Party leader in 1975 and was Prime Minister from 1979 to 1990, when she oversaw the Falklands conflict and inspired the resurgence of satire,

which was christened 'alternative comedy'. Socialist firebrands such as Ben Elton became stars during her reign, using their success to buy some rather nice property and make musicals with Andrew Lloyd Webber. Ninety per cent of London taxi drivers would like Lady Thatcher back as Prime Minister, and nearly all carry a small shrine to her in the boot of their cabs.

THOMAS, DYLAN

This Swansea-born poet and playwright is the Welsh answer to Shakespeare and Burns, though his lifestyle was more akin to that of a modern rock star: he drank and drugged himself into an early grave at the age of 39 and finally passed out at New York's Chelsea Hotel. He is alleged to have said, '18 straight whiskies; I think it's a record' to the barman shortly before his collapse, which showed him to be part of the proud heritage of British binge drinkers. Thomas is most well known for his play *Under Milk Wood*, a mix of dark wit and wonderfully poetic wordiness that is set in the fictional Welsh village of Llareggub, a name which the BBC obviously didn't take the time to read backwards before commissioning the work as a radio play starring Richard Burton. Burton went on to star in the film version of the play with Elizabeth Taylor.

TIMES CROSSWORD

An institution regularly tackled by great Brits such as Winston Churchill and Great Uncle Bulgaria, the *Times* crossword was introduced in 1930 and has become an

integral part of the day for many. Its cryptic format demands concentration and dedication, which is what led the newspaper to claim that it has the power to stave off Alzheimer's disease and mental deterioration in the elderly. A completed *Times* crossword should always be held with the page folded outwards to show just how clever you are. Hopefully no one will have noticed that you have just filled in most of the squares with obscenities.

TIT TUESDAY
Only denied national holiday status by its ever-shifting nature, Tit Tuesday is the first official day of British Summertime. This is marked by all males between the ages of 18 and 65 standing outside the pub and enjoying a refreshing beverage while marvelling at what British women have been concealing beneath coats, jackets and cardigans all through the winter. Despite its name, Tit Tuesday need not fall on a Tuesday. The UN reports that climate change means that Tit Tuesday is happening an average of two days earlier every year.

TIZER
One of Britain's favourite red, carbonated, sugary drinks, Tizer was marketed in the 1970s as 'Tizer the Appetizer', which saw confused restaurateurs across the land removing prawn cocktails from their menus in favour of the mystery-flavoured drink. Being ahead of its time this didn't catch on, though Pepsi is now considered as a suitable starter at

fried chicken outlets. Designed to be drunk warm with a wasp in it, Tizer is produced by Scottish manufacturer A G Barr PLC, who also produce Irn Bru (*see* IRN BRU), though it was initially launched in 1924 in Manchester.

TORREMOLINOS
This colony in the south of Spain, the name of which translates as 'smell of sunburn', was established in 1974, during what was known as the *Y Viva Espana* invasion. British tourists, disguised in sun hats, and some wearing castanets, took the city from the Spanish to establish what later became known as The Four Elements of Continental British Tourism: beans, bitter, bacon, black pudding. Bitter was replaced as one of the elements in 1981, when lager was finally declared a suitable drink for heterosexual men by an Act of Parliament. Initially, there were violent clashes between the indigenous populations and the occupying forces, but an accord was later reached whereby the Spanish agreed the Brits were the hardest and the Spanish could lace the copious amounts of malt vinegar that the Brits use (*see* FISH AND CHIPS) with urine. A limit on the number of sovereign rings that ex-pat Brits can wear was imposed in 1998, when it was discovered that the resort was starting to sink under their weight. Torremolinos is the number one spot that Brits emigrate to in order to escape what they see as an overload of immigrants arriving in the UK. They always do so without irony and without bothering to learn Spanish.

TOWER OF LONDON

A world heritage site and one of our most famed tourist attractions, the Tower of London is the home of the Crown Jewels and well known for its links to royal incarcerations and executions. Elizabeth I was imprisoned there and Ann Boleyn and Lady Jane Grey were both executed there. In modern times this would mean that the whole site of these grisly deaths would be pulled down and a memorial garden would be built, rather than allow it to become a hugely popular tourist site. Legend has is that the presence of ravens at the site is essential for the survival of the Tower, the monarchy and even Britain itself . So terrorists looking to destroy our great nation should probably invest less in hydrogen peroxide and flying lessons and more in finding out what kills ravens quickly and efficiently.

TOWN CRIERS

Initially a way of spreading messages to the populace in towns and provinces, these local announcers of laws and news are recorded as far back as the early sixteenth century. In modern Britain the position of town crier is reserved for loud men with an overblown sense of self-importance and who hanker to wear tights in public places. Now that this is a largely ceremonial role, town criers often compete against each other in national and international competitions to see who can bellow 'Oh yez!' the loudest. Ideas to modernise this element of British history have included having rappers ape the news-spreading techniques of their

tricorn hat-wearing forebears, with 'Yo bitches!' replacing the traditional greeting.

TRUCULENCE

This is a highly combative character trait that made all of those bits of the atlas turn pink (who on earth chose that colour?) back in our empire building days (*see* EMPIRE), but also got us through World War I and the sequel, World War II – *The Bosh Strikes Back*. It also helped England win the World Cup in 1966 and little Archie Gemmil score against the Dutch in 1978. Originally thought to be a uniquely working-class characteristic (*see* CLASS), and often aided by a pint of gin, a quart of mild or similarly imperial measure of alcohol, the truculent gene has proved itself to be socially mobile in the twenty-first century. Middle-class parents now apply the same never-say-die attitude to obtaining school places for their offspring and in defence of their need for a 4x4.

THE TUBE

Several British cities have their own underground or metro system, but it is the London Underground that is the greatest of these by far, with 253 miles of track and 275 stations served by the Tube's trains. The Tube map itself is a design classic, imagined in the style of a wiring diagram by Underground worker Harry Beck. This design has since been copied for similar networks the world over. In 1974 a new, updated version of the diagrammatic Tube map had to

be withdrawn as it was inadvertently designed in such a way that it could be used to negotiate the London Underground or build a basic nuclear reactor. London Underground is a favoured suicide destination for many Britons, which means that the often traumatised staff who work on the system have had to come up with inventive ways of describing suicide-induced delays to the running of trains. It is said that London Underground staff have more euphemisms for pointless death than minor celebrities have for cocaine. Favoured excuses for delays include 'due to a person being taken ill at Baker Street', 'due to an incident at Pimlico' and 'due to severed limbs on the track at Kentish Town'. You should always avoid eye contact with anyone on the Tube, as London tradition says that you must fight anyone who manages to catch your gaze.

TUNNOCK'S

Responsible for some of Britain's sweetest foodstuffs, the Scottish baker Tunnock's has been keeping dentists in work since 1890 (*see* TEETH). Their popular range of marshmallow and caramel-based snacks includes the much-celebrated Tunnock's Tea Cake, the Caramel Wafer and the delightfully gooey Snowball, all of which have been tuck shop and lunchbox fodder for generations. The quiet, unfussy nature of the business and the retro feel of the products that it manufactures has lead to a cult following for the company, which claims to sell 4 million of its Caramel Wafers a week. Scientists predict that the Scottish people

will be 4 per cent marshmallow by 2050 and possibly have a crispy wafer-like skin.

2-TONE

This was the last British fashion to make British youth take to the dancefloor *and* dress smartly. It was also the first to really make a feature of Britain's growing ethnic mix, with the 2-Tone logos mixing black and white in the same way that they were mixed in the bands which made up the movement. At a time of political and racial tension bands like The Specials, Selecter and Bad Manners proved the idiocy of racists, as skinheads came to their concerts, danced to the music and then made Nazi salutes at the stage where a group of black and white musicians were playing for them. Many of these racist fans of ska still insist that the upbeat reggae was actually invented by Lonnie Donnegan and Cliff Richard but was stolen by black immigrants coming over here and taking our musical styles.

UMBRELLAS

A Briton without an umbrella is like a Frenchman without a string of onions around his neck or a Russian who has not passed out on the floor in a pool of vodka, that is to say it is simply unimaginable. From the city gent's tightly furled full-length brolly to the see-through plastic canopy of a child, our umbrellas give out unspoken signals about our taste, status and character. Opening an umbrella indoors is said to be unlucky, though perhaps it is not as unlucky as being killed with ricin poison administered by umbrella, which is what happened to exiled Bulgarian journalist Georgi Makov in 1978. The assassination took place on Waterloo Bridge and is said to have performed by an agent of the Bulgarian communist government, of which Makov was a critic. The agent obviously saw the umbrella as the innocent British icon that no one would ever suspect of carrying a deadly poison.

UNDERSTATEMENT

As we are a nation of few emotions, visitors have to learn to read between the lines. For example, 'No, it's fine' actually

means 'This meal is inedible' and 'I think it is just a scratch' translates as 'The Hun seem to have blown my leg clean off'. This also means that it is very hard to spot the Brit in a state of anger. Those unfamiliar with our ways should watch out for the phrase 'Would you mind awfully?', which is our equivalent of the American-English expression 'Do the fuck what I say right now or I'll put a cap in your ass, motherfucker'.

UNION FLAG

The flag of Britain has been mired in controversy since a version was first introduced in 1606. The flag we fly now has been in use since 1801: St George's cross represents England in the design, St Andrew's saltire for Scotland and the St Patrick's saltire is for Northern Ireland. Obviously there should be a bloody great red dragon in the middle to represent Wales, but that would make a right mess of the design, so we just think about them instead, like we would think about a distant auntie who sends us gift tokens at Christmas but who we never meet. The red, white and blue colours of the flag are generally accepted to signify Britishness, yet the display of the flag is often seen as signifying far right-wing views. This is because the national symbol was hijacked by extremist groups such as the National Front in the 1970s. The name of the flag itself is controversial, and many refer to it as the Union Jack, even though this is generally the name for the flag when it is flown at sea. In order to be hung correctly the broad white

band of the Scots saltire should be above the red of the saltire of St Patrick at the side nearest the flagpole. Those wearing Union Flag boxer shorts should always dress to the left.

UNSWERVING OPTIMISM
Whether it is the undying belief that our national teams will qualify for international football tournaments (*see* MATHE-MATICAL POSSIBILITY), the idea that we will score any points in the Eurovision Song Contest or the notion that 'it will all be over by Christmas', we Brits are always willing to believe that things will turn out right in the end. Obviously things do not always work that way, but this belief that Britain is right and that Britain has the right, does help us endure hard times and come out on top eventually. This characteristic is best seen in the endless stream of young Brits willing to queue for the chance of appearing on *Big Brother* in the belief that even being voted out in week two will lead to fame and a lengthy career in the media.

VAT

This optional tax marks Britain out as one of the most forward-thinking nations when it comes to fiscal matters. It may be levied at a hefty 17.5 per cent, but VAT (Value Added Tax) is voluntary for both customer and business in many situations, with only social conscience helping us decide whether or not the transaction should incur the charge. VAT-optional purchases include many of those in the building trade, where buyers should ask for the 'best price' and possibly add a wink or a rubbing together of the thumb and forefinger to be sure of being understood. Some restaurants run special VAT-free days (at least for the business), which are denoted by a sign on the till saying 'Card machine out of order, cash only'. *The author would like to point out that he always pays VAT, sometimes throwing in an extra 25 per cent or so just to be nice.

VESTA

Before every town centre boasted a Chinese and an Indian restaurant or takeaway there was simply Vesta. Named after

the Roman god of rehydration, the exotic ethnic foodstuffs became a supermarket staple in the 1970s, bringing spicy glamour to a period of culinary austerity. The Vesta brand introduced many Britons to curry, as well as wowing them with the wonderfully curly crispy noodles that accompanied its chow mein meal. Naturally, Brits were disappointed when actual ethnic restaurants appeared in their towns; they paled into significance against the more authentic Vesta taste. Vesta products are still available in supermarkets and plans are currently afoot to send crates of the dehydrated food out to China and India so that chefs there can learn to make curry and chow mein correctly.

VESTS

There is nothing more unedifying than the sight of a British man wearing a string vest on a foreign beach; the attendant chicken wire tan/sunburn effect the day after is really something to show off by the pool. These surprisingly efficient under-garments have been warming and cooling our men for many years, but have fallen out of fashion in recent years, as has the simple cotton vest. Most men now prefer to wear plain T-shirts beneath a shirt, though such garments on children do not allow for the ritual humiliation of being forced to play in pants and vest if they forget their games kit. Vests are still popular with the proprietors of bed and breakfast hotels and are traditionally worn with an egg stain down the front. Americans call vests 'wifebeaters' – a colloquial term *we* use for a brand of lager.

VICARS

Though priests are popular with the Catholic population and those investigating sexual misdemeanours, the vicar is a truly British figurehead of religion. That is to say they are generally considered to be unthreatening figures of fun, bumbling and just about up to conducting a wedding, funeral or christening. The vicar is often a central figure in sitcoms, with *The Vicar of Dibley* being one recent example. Our respect for men of the cloth is shown by the fact that they are one of the main choices for men when it comes to fancy dress, making the tarts and vicars party a popular themed evening. This popularity may have a small amount to do with mocking the propensity of members of the clergy to embroil themselves in scandal, but it has far more to do with the fact that men hate fancy dress. Most men, however, do own a pair of black trousers and a black shirt, together with a willingness to don them accessorised with a small white strip of card at the neck if it means they get a chance to see a large number of women dressed as tarts.

VILLAGES

As our urban environment becomes increasingly Americanised and genericised, with many town centres looking nearly identical, it falls to our villages to retain all that is individual and special about the British way of life. A proper village should have a pub, church, village green and, preferably, a duck pond. To maintain an authentic village bloodline there should be no breeding with those who do

not live in the village. After all, a graveyard with more than three family names looks chaotic and unruly. Outsiders should be treated with suspicion, especially those who buy holiday homes in the village. Greetings such as: 'Oh, you're from London. I went there once. Didn't like it', should be used at all opportunities.

V-SIGN

Whichever way you wave yours, the V-sign is a huge part of our culture. Winston Churchill was famous for showing the V for victory during World War II, though he was often seen using it with his palm facing inwards, which is our way of saying 'fuck you'. Less crude than the American single-digit version, this sign is at its best when waved from the window of a car at a fellow motorist who has committed some minor transgression against your personal motoring code. For proper effect, the V-sign should be quickly shown and then withdrawn with a snap of the wrist. This is known as 'flipping the Vs'.

W

WANKER

This is our most unique swear word, being so far outside mainstream understanding in most other English-speaking nations that it was snuck into an episode *of The Simpsons* with no outcry. Had the show used the US equivalent 'jerk-off' then it would have been cut from the episode. Australians do use the word, but they change its initial insulting meaning and turn it into a verb that means drunk. 'I am wankered, they are wankered, we are wankered'. Yes, we get the idea: the whole country is completely pissed 90 per cent of the time. Well done. The word 'wanker' should be used as a term of abuse and preferably accompanied by the correct hand signal, which replicates the act of male masturbation. The term can also be used as a term of affection upon meeting a friend, as in 'How are you, you old wanker?'.

WAR GAMES

'Da-la-la-la' goes the sound of a small boy machine-gunning his school friends in the playground at morning break. Unlike similar scenarios in the US, the British boy is playing

and it is an invisible, imaginary semi-automatic weapon that is cradled in his arms. As we are so good at war it is only natural that children wish to act out our famous victories during their playtime, with the least popular children being forced to play the Germans, the Argentinians or some allied troops coming under friendly fire. For a generation raised on playing war, reading *Battle* or *Commando* this urge to play war continues into adult life and many join historical re-enactment groups or war-gaming societies. Some, though simply hang around outside football grounds wearing Stone Island jumpers saying 'Jog on' a lot and arranging dust-ups with other divorced fathers-of-three via their mobile phones.

WARM BEER
Contrary to the beliefs of some visitors and even some natives, when we Britons talk of warm beer, we don't mean something that has been heated up in a microwave oven before being served or cans that have been left out in the sun. We simply mean proper British beer that is served at or just below room temperature and which can therefore, like good wine, be savoured when a good gulp hits the taste buds (*see* ALE). Australian lager brand Fosters, who exported their beer to the UK in revenge for all the convicts we sent the other way, advertise their antipodean brew with the slogan 'Well, you wouldn't want a warm beer', though personally I would rather down the tepid urine of Peter Andre than drink Fosters. Not that I do imbibe Mr Andre's waste fluids, you understand.

WEATHER

There is a theory that we simply would not converse with each other were it not for the British weather and the opportunities for conversation that it throws up, such as 'Looks like rain', 'Rain again today' and 'I told you we shouldn't have bought this executive home on a flood plain'. The weather in the UK ranges from too cold to too hot and too wet to too dry; approximately four days in mid-May are reasonable and completely unworthy of comment.

WHISKY

Citizens of other countries may be able to put forward decent (though obviously fallacious) arguments about how their homelands outrank Britain in terms of the advancement of engineering, the discovery of cures for life-threatening illnesses or even the production of pop music, but not one can claim to be anywhere close when it comes to spirits. Scotch whisky is the default drink dispensed when you ask for whisky almost anywhere in the world and its hundreds of varieties drive the Whisky Trail tourism in the Highlands and the need for drying-out centres in the major cities. Distilled from water and malted barley, Scotch whisky is thought to have been in production for as long as 1,500 years; Resolve, Alka Seltzer and Irn Bru (*see* IRN BRU) were invented just after the secrets of distilling were brought to Scotland by monks. Some Brits prefer Irish whiskey, which has an 'e' in, by which I mean the name has

a letter 'e' that Scotch is missing, not that it has an ecstasy tablet in it, though some pubs in Essex do offer the drink this way. Irish whiskey is mostly made in Southern Ireland, although the Old Bushmills Distillery is in Northern Ireland.

WHITE CLIFFS OF DOVER

'There'll be bluebirds over the White Cliffs of Dover,' sang Dame Vera Lynn in her prescient wartime song about the potential effects of global warming. The bluebird is a native of the Americas, but could soon breed in Kent if Dame Vera's predictions are correct. The White Cliffs are very much a symbol of coming back to Blighty, of spying those precipices and feeling a warmth and love for home. It can also signify that your booze cruise is over and you should at least try to look sober, as you may have to explain that those 240 crates of lager are for personal use only and that you really don't know how those two Chinese gentlemen got into that secret panel in the back of your van.

WIMBLEDON

The annual Grand Slam tournament at the All England Lawn Tennis and Croquet Club is one of the major events in our sporting calendar and is used by many as a reminder of when not to book a holiday in Britain, as rain (*see* RAIN) is always guaranteed for its two-week duration. This period is also the only fortnight in the year when anyone becomes remotely interested in purchasing barley water, which is a drink for

those who find orange squash a little too exciting. Since time immemorial, menopausal women have gathered on Henman Hill during the tournament to repeat the incantation 'Cumontim', which is believed to be an ancient prayer for a British victory in battle. The last British singles winner was Virginia Wade, back in 1977, and Fred Perry (*see* PERRY, FRED) was the last men's singles winner in 1936. Fans will often queue overnight for a chance to purchase one of the day tickets for the centre court, and some use the time to sell sexual favours in order to be able to afford to purchase the traditional strawberries and cream.

WIMPY

It is frightfully British that our introduction to the never-ending tide of American-influenced branded fast food should come on a proper plate and be accompanied some-what confusingly, by a knife and fork. Wimpy bars were a step up from the frothy coffee houses and offered a strange selection of burgers and sausages served with chips, with many dishes not being too alien to those more familiar with the menu at the greasy spoon café. Wimpy was loved for its enormous milkshakes, though it was also famed for exotic desserts like the Brown Derby, which always looked intriguing but sounded far too scatological for most teenagers to order. It turns out it was just a doughnut with some ice cream and chocolate sauce on top. Why didn't they just say that? Wimpy bars still exist in towns where time has stood still since 1973.

WORKING MEN'S CLUBS

These shrines to sticky carpets, cheap beer and nicotine-stained old folk are a declining part of British life. As traditional trades and industry die out, so the leisure facilities built for those workforces are starting to be sold off and redeveloped. Some still hold out though, instantly taking visitors back to a period when brown decor was considered to be quite racy and when smoking 40 cigarettes a day was seen as giving the lungs a good workout. Various schemes have been mooted to help save these traditionally male environments. Suggestions include opening them up to a wider range of social classes or even turning some into middle-class men's clubs, where like-minded souls can discuss status anxiety over a reasonable Merlot while watching news on house prices, without the possibility of being confronted by anyone with a threateningly large knowledge of gas boilers.

WORLD WAR II

There can barely be a Briton alive who does not feel the hairs on his or her neck stand on end when hearing the speech that Winston Churchill made as a prelude to the Battle of Britain, speaking of the struggle to come and the spirit that would be needed. The speech concluded: '...if the British Empire and its Commonwealth last for a thousand years, men will still say, "This was their finest hour".' This term 'finest hour' has come to represent the whole of World War II, with some justification. Everyone's lives changed.

Many didn't survive to see victory and Britain at peace again. This was a pivotal moment in our history. World War II disproved the theory that a sequel was never as good as the original, retaining top spot over World War I to this day. Without it we wouldn't have had *Dad's Army*, Action Man, *Battle* comic or that brief, awkward period where we had to be all pally with the Russians and pretend that Communism was good. The war taught us a lot about ourselves, about community and about how to pretend that parsnips tasted a bit like bananas. It also gave us enough material to keep the British film industry alive well into the 1960s.

XENOPHOBIA

The natural state of Britons, perhaps due to the number of invasions we have suffered during our history, is one of fear and suspicion of anything or anyone foreign. We fear the Germans because they might invade, the French because they seem a bit frisky and a good number of Britons fear anyone more than a shade darker than pasty-white because they are probably richer than us, as they have to spend less on bronzing lotions and sunscreen. Xenophobia is, at its root, probably a healthy defense reflex, though it is often confused with racism, which is not. The British form of xenophobia is more about the dislike of French markets in our town centres selling overpriced bread and olives than any real hatred of the French people. Sentences containing the words 'coming over here, taking our' tend to be a signifier of racism as do sentences beginning 'You know what's wrong with this country?' when said by taxi drivers or any middle-aged comedian who constantly moans that they can't get on television anymore 'because of political correctness'.

X FACTOR

Created by concentrating all the inherent evil of shows like *Pop Idol, Stars in Their Eyes* and that rubbish one from the BBC that no one can remember, *X Factor* has now sucked up and spat out almost 70 per cent of the population. Rumour has it that Simon Cowell et al have actually instigated a secret breeding scheme to ensure that they have enough willing contestants for future episodes. Should the show be cancelled then this genetically engineered strain of morons will be used as organic cavity insulation in an upcoming series of *Grand Designs*. The Liberal Democrats are toying with the controversial idea of adopting a policy that would see the *X Factor* model of voting adopted in Parliamentary elections, meaning that only teenage girls, gay men and women over the age of 65 will be allowed into polling stations.

X-RAY

It may be a German invention, but it has taken British minds to truly appreciate the commercial application of the X-ray. This ingenuity has allowed us to realise that an X-ray is an essential part of any claim made on our behalf by the growing number of no-win, no-fee accident lawyers that advertise on daytime television. Those able to drag themselves away from *The Jeremy Kyle Show* long enough to get dressed can make a decent income from slinging themselves over a wonky paving stone or scything off a limb on a supermarket trolley. Guidelines on hospital waiting times

now mean that you can fracture a tibia outside the chip shop, get X-rayed and still be home in time to catch children's TV.

YARD OF ALE

This supremely imperial measurement of alcohol was once said to be under threat by the EU-imposed 'metre of lager', but the Brussels Eurocrats soon realised that no other nation could down such a significant amount of booze in one go and hence left the tradition unchanged. The yard of ale, served in a long glass with a round bowl at the bottom, is traditionally drunk on significant birthdays or stag nights (*see* STAG NIGHTS). Under no circumstances should the ale be substituted by Malibu, carrot juice or your own urine.

YBAs

The YBAs (Young British Artists) dominated the contemporary art world in the 1990s with their combination of brashness and unconventional conceptual art. Tracey Emin, Damien Hirst, Sarah Lucas and Rachel Whiteread were as likely to be on the news pages as the arts pages of newspapers with all their sawing-dirty-pants-in-half and preserving-them-in-formaldehyde-style japes. Named after

a series of exhibitions at the Saatchi Gallery, the YBAs upset everybody, especially those who cared very little about art. 'This is not art,' the offended cried as they admired their poster of that tennis player scratching her arse. Many of the YBAs are now millionaires, as is the bloke who took the photo of the tennis player scratching her arse, or at least he should be if there is any justice in the world.

YELLOW LINES

Parking has become something of an obsession in Britain over the last ten years: many of us now have to pay to park outside our own houses and privately employed parking wardens stop us from actually moving our cars to anywhere that might be vaguely useful. The addition of red routes, bus lanes and speed cameras means that it is nearly impossible to drive to the newsagent at the bottom of the street for a packet of cigarettes without incurring some kind of fine. At this current level of escalation, even the workers who paint on yellow lines will not be able to find anywhere legal to park their vans by 2015, with park-and-ride schemes being set up in Calais for those who wish to do any Christmas shopping in London.

Y-FRONTS

Before model Nick Kamen inspired the boxer short revolution by undressing in an advert for Levi's in 1985 there was only one kind of underwear that a British man would countenance and that was the Y-front. This patriotic

garment was available in a greying off-white or a kind of institutional blue and could only be purchased at Marks and Spencer, though on special occasions, such as Christmas or Valentine's Day, the store made limited editions of other colours available, such as brown-and-tan or orange. The boxer boom left men confused and uncomfortable, eventually leading to calls for lessons in the correct wearing of the imported trend to be added to the National Curriculum as well as being offered freely as evening classes. Y-fronts are still available and can last a single man for up to eight days if worn correctly (four of those days being inside-out). Political cartoonist Steve Bell often portrayed Prime Minister John Major as being the type of man who would wear outsized Y-fronts. Bell himself is said to prefer the thong.

YOBS

Derived from nineteenth-century back slang for 'boy', the word yob is used to define young men (and, more recently, women) whose behaviour is seen as beyond the pale (*see* HOODIES). This group used to be made up exclusively of working-class youths from whichever youth cult was threatening society most at the time, but this perception has now widened to a belief in a 'yob culture' in Britain that can include all ages and all classes, including vodka-snorting royals. In order to counter the negative impact of this breakdown in civility, the government are looking at plans to put a positive spin on things by naming a City of Yob Culture. Swansea, Liverpool and Corby are set to fight it

out (possibly literally) for the inaugural title. The results will be announced live on the Yob Channel, with citizens of the winning city being awarded free premium lager for a year, which will replace the water in their taps.

Z

ZERO TOLERANCE

Often quoted as the solution to inner city crime, zero tolerance has certainly worked in some parts of the US, where even the most trivial breaches of the law are pounced upon and dealt with. This policy sounds all very well when argued for on phone-in radio programmes (*see* SHOCK JOCKS), but it simply goes against British nature. In Britain we prefer to be extremely tolerant to an unspecified level at which point we break and all hell lets loose. This 'be polite about it until you blow' approach can range from our efforts at international diplomacy to neighbour disputes ('That is the last time those kids will be kicking the ball against our wall. Darling, fetch me the baseball bat').

Z-LIST

Consisting mostly of *Big Brother* flotsam, royal family floor scrapings and the offspring of C-list celebrities, the Z-list is the place to go if you want to add some 'glamour' to your sandwich shop opening, jumble sale or exhibition of amateur pornography. Mostly on probation for serial oxygen thievery,

these prime examples of Britain's wannabe culture are used as fillers in gossip magazines on weeks when there is a shortage of shots of C-list cellulite or B-list singers out shopping. The Z-list is the place that shopping channel presenters aspire to be.

ZOOPHILIA

Men from Wales are often accused of taking part in inter-species relations and their country's many sheep are usually the alleged subject of their affections, though these cries of 'sheep shagger' usually come from men who think nothing of taking an inflatable sheep sex-doll to a major sporting competition in order to taunt their near neighbours. It makes you wonder which of those men has sex with sheep most on their mind, really. The British are known to be a nation of animal lovers, but anything approaching heavy petting with another species is generally frowned upon (especially in a public swimming pool, where it is seen on a par with bombing, running or smoking).

How British Are You?

This quiz will test your knowledge of how well you know the land you live in and the British way of life. You can use it to see what you have learned by reading *We're British, Innit* or simply pass it to your mates and see how well they can do without reading the book. Answer enough questions correctly and you can wrap yourself in the flag, get too many wrong and we'll send Richard Littlejohn round to pack your bags. Think of it as the Citizenship Test for those who already consider themselves citizens or a primer for those who want to be. The details of the answers can be found in the main body of the book and the page number where you can find this information is printed below each question.

1. Mushy peas is a traditional British dish that is made from:
 A. Marrowfat peas.
 B. Garden peas.
 C. Avocado.
 See Mushy peas; page 123

2. Winston Churchill referred to his bouts of depression as his:
 A. Black dog.
 B. Guide dog.

C. Nodding dog.

See Churchill, Winston; page 36

3. *Readers' Wives* is:

A. A magazine of amateur pornography, to which men send in naked pictures of their wives.

B. The annual summer poetry supplement to *The Spectator* magazine, with contributions from the spouses of subscribers.

C. The Christmas ball held each year for the partners of those in the publishing industry in London.

See Readers' Wives; page 162

4. The last words of Admiral Lord Nelson were:

A. Rub, rub.

B. Kiss me Hardy.

C. Kismet Hardy.

See Nelson; page 130

5. The presenter of *Autumnwatch* is:

A. Bill Oddie.

B. Donal McIntyre.

C. Kerry Katona.

See Autumnwatch/Springwatch; page 12

6. Irn Bru is:

A. A soft drink manufactured in Scotland.

B. A vitamin supplement manufactured in Wales.

C. A Viagra competitor manufactured in Northern Ireland.

See Irn Bru; page 100

7. St George is believed to have been born in:
 A. Turkey.
 B. England.
 C. Scotland.

 See St George; page 174

8. The Blitz Spirit refers to:
 A. The community cohesion during bombing raids in World War II.
 B. The New Romantic scene in Soho in the early 1980s.
 C. Illegal bathtub gin manufactured during the 1940s.

 See Blitz Spirit; page 20

9. Norman Tebbit's 'cricket test' refers to:
 A. Whether second-generation immigrants support the team from their place of birth or their parents' place of birth.
 B. How long an immigrant must have lived in the UK before he can play sport at international level for a British nation.
 C. Whether or not you can keep a bat under your bed to deal with intruders.

 See Cricket test; page 44

10. A Hornby is:

 A. A middle-class, Johnny-come-lately football fan.

 B. A model-railway enthusiast.

 C. A traditional beer-barrel maker.

 See Hornbies; page 94

11. The Bowler hat was first designed to be worn for:

 A. Horse riding.

 B. Cricket.

 C. Weddings.

 See Bowler hats; page 24

12. The full correct name for the British flag is:

 A. The Union Flag.

 B. The Union Jack.

 C. The British Standard.

 See entry on page 203

13. Does the phrase 'innit' usually mean?

 A. What I am saying is unquestionably true, sir. Do not doubt my certainty in the facts I have explained to you.

 B. What I am saying is a joke.

 C. To be inside something, like a youth custody centre.

 See Innit; page 99

14. Did gender-bending blancmange-faced pop star Boy George famously declare that he would prefer a cup of tea to:
 A. Sex?
 B. Another hit single?
 C. An invite to Elton John's wedding?
 See Tea; page 190

15. An amateur is:
 A. Someone who does something purely out of the spirit of enjoyment.
 B. Someone who is not very good at something.
 C. Someone who neither charges for it or is any good at it; a bit like your ex.
 See Amateurism; page 7

16. Baked beans are made from tomato sauce and which kind of bean?
 A. Haricot beans.
 B. Kidney beans.
 C. Magic beans.
 See Baked beans; page 14

17. Someone stands on your foot while you are travelling on the bus. Should you:
 A. Apologise profusely.
 B. Demand an apology.
 C. Punch them hard in the face.
 See entry on page 9

18. The term Ordnance Survey refers to:

 A. The vast range of maps that show the British Isles in various scales.

 B. The results of a random sampling of what arms schoolchildren carry with them.

 C. An organisation that carries out opinion polls.

See entry on page 134

19. What is a haggis?

 A. A mixture of offal, oats and onions which is contained in a sheep's stomach.

 B. A small mammal that is hunted in the Scottish Highlands during the winter months.

 C. A droning musical instrument that originated in Dundee.

See Haggis; page 87

20. What were the denominations of pre-decimal currency used in Britain?

 A. Pounds, shillings and pence.

 B. Fathoms, leagues and knots.

 C. Rocks, pebbles and gravel.

See Old money; page 133

21. The gin and tonic was invented:

 A. As a way of getting troops in India to take quinine.

 B. As a means of using up an accidental over-production of gin.

C. To make a spirit associated with toothless Victorian binge drinkers palatable to the middle classes.

See Gin and tonic; page 77

22. The name Boudica refers to:
 A. A warrior queen who was the scourge of the Roman invaders.
 B. A religious leader who brought Christianity to Britain.
 C. A nightclub in Romford.

See Boudica; page 24

23. Which of the following condiments is not a suitable thing to put on your chips?
 A. Balsamic vinegar.
 B. Malt vinegar.
 C. Acetic acid.

See Fish and chips; page 65

24. The phrase most associated with Rich Tea biscuits is:
 A. A drink's too wet without one.
 B. We make' em, you dunk 'em.
 C. Buy some chocolate Hob Nobs, you cheapskate.

See Rich Tea biscuits; page 165

25. What is special about the day known as Tit Tuesday?
 A. It is the first day of summer, as denoted by female office workers who remove their jumpers and cardigans to reveal their curves.

B. It is the day that the RSPB hold their annual survey of British garden birds.

C. It is the day that marks the start of a new television series by popular comedian Dom Joly.

See Tit Tuesday; page 196

MOSTLY As

Well done. You know your stuff. Break out the suet pudding and some rhubarb and custard sweets before you hang out some bunting and enjoy a pint of real ale or a bucket of Pimms. Take the day off and polish up your Sovereign rings or simply tune into Radio 4 and enjoy a cucumber sandwich in the rain while you laugh at the entries you know and recognise in *We're British, Innit.*

MOSTLY Bs

Not bad, but you could do with brushing up on your Britishness. Try a Marmite and Ovaltine diet for the next week. These brain foods should help you absorb all the information in *We're British, Innit* and leave you feeling wonderfully British. At the end of the week reward yourself with some pie and mash or fish and chips before apologising profusely to everyone for no apparent reason.

MOSTLY Cs

Hang your head in shame and leave the country. Either you have been overdoing the binge drinking or you are a Peruvian tourist. You probably don't even know how to say 'Leicester' properly or which Spice Girl is which. Be sure to read *We're British, Innit* from cover to cover to discover the real truth about Britain and its ways.

Acknowledgements

This book would not have been possible without the wonderful people of Britain and especially the assortment of oddballs and fruitcakes I am proud to call my friends. Thanks especially to Christina Lamb for not becoming overly annoyed at the build up of both dirty mugs and increasingly ridiculous puns, to my agent Susan Smith at MBA for occasionally sending me rude pictures to inspire me and to Claire Kingston and all at HarperCollins for their enthusiasm and willingness to discuss white dog excrement at length.

Gratitude for suggestions for entries, purchase of beverages and general help or inspiration must go to Chris Butler, Tom Hodgkinson, Susie Hollands, Bee Lavender, Gita Malhotra, Matthew McCarthy, Johnny Nigma, Mickey Penguin, Graham Pond, P3, Ian Vince, Boff Whalley and Mike Wyeld.

Thanks for reading. You can find out more about me at www.iainaitch.com.

Index

Note: entries in **bold** refer to main headings.

Beautiful People

A CHARMING AND FUNNY MEMOIR OF ESCAPING
A BONKERS FAMILY AND FOLLOWING YOUR DREAMS

Simon Doonan's childhood was a curious mix of small town boredom and bright light city dreams. Growing up in a working-class area of Reading with the madcap Doonan clan – Mother Betty, Father Terry, blind Aunt Phyllis, grandmother Narg and Grandfather D.C. – he yearned to get out and find the Beautiful People whom he imagined lived fabulous lives of glitz and glamour.

This is the charming and funny story of how Simon eventually finds a way out and escapes to London with best friend Biddie Biddlecombe. Along the way they stumble upon punks, drunks, ladies of the night, the long arm of the law and all sorts of camps, vamps and outrageous scamps.

But does he ever find the Beautiful People? Or could they be the ones he left behind...?

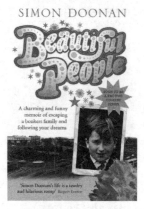

ISBN 978-0-00-726954-9

In all good bookshops from May 2008

To order this title please call our Customer Hotline number.

Tel: 0870 787 1724 • Fax: 0870 787 1725

CREDIT CARDS ACCEPTED

For further information about other books from Collins please visit

www.collins.co.uk

There's A Hippo In My Cistern

ONE MAN'S MISADVENTURES ON THE ECO-FRONTLINE

The hilarious true-life tale of one man's journey from self-confessed planet-killing lad to eco-friendly, green-crusader Dad set against the backdrop of Cool Britannia, Blair's Britain and the rise of the green movement.

Back in the nineties, *Loaded* journalist, Pete May was your normal twenty-something male: a football mad, beer guzzling, Dr Who watching lad's lad, quite happy surrounding himself with countless pizza boxes, beer cans and other environmentally unfriendly consumer items. Recycling to Pete was a debate about whether he should turn his socks inside out and reuse them.

Then one day, out of nowhere, along came eco bunny Nicola – a greener than green environmental activist. Could two people so different really fall for each other? Would Pete ever change his ways and sign up to the green lifestyle?

This is the charming and funny true-life tale of one man's struggle to grapple with the good life, go green and get the girl.

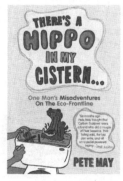

ISBN 978-0-00-726431-5

Getting Into Guinness

**A QUIRKY HISTORY OF THE MANY MADCAP ATTEMPTS TO
GET INTO *THE GUINNESS BOOK OF RECORDS* TOLD BY A MAN
DETERMINED TO SET HIS OWN WORLD RECORD**

When Larry Olmstead decided to get into Guinness by setting a new world record, he began to wonder about all those people who had gone before him.

Now a household name, *The Guinness Book Of World Records* has a rich and varied history full of hilarious record breaking attempts and fiercely determined people.

Now, for the first time, Larry Olmstead takes you behind the records to learn about the colourful characters who set them. Meet the Frenchman Michael Lotito who won the title of greatest omnivore for his ability to eat up to 2 pounds of metal a day (he's even eaten a supermarket trolley), or find out about the oldest vomit (160 million years)!

This is the hilarious true story of the quirkiest, most memorable records and one man's attempts to join them by setting his very own world record.

ISBN 978-0-00-726129-1

In all good bookshops from October 2008

To order this title please call our Customer Hotline number.

Tel: 0870 787 1724 • Fax: 0870 787 1725

CREDIT CARDS ACCEPTED

For further information about other books from Collins please visit

www.collins.co.uk